SpringerBriefs in Education

Open and Distance Education

Series Editors

Olaf Zawacki-Richter, University of Oldenburg, Oldenburg, Niedersachsen, Germany

Junhong Xiao, Shantou Radio & Television University, Shantou, Guangdong, China

Editorial Board

Trisha Craig, Yale-NUS College, Singapore, Singapore

Ursula Glunk, University College Freiburg, University of Freiburg, Freiburg im Breisgau, Baden-Württemberg, Germany

You Guo Jiang, Boston College, Chestnut Hill, MA, USA

Rui Yang, Faculty of Education, University of Hong Kong, Hong Kong, Hong Kong

Akiyoshi Yonezawa, Tohoku University, Sendai, Japan

Developing human capital through education and training is crucial to social and economic progress. However despite efforts to achieve equity and learning opportunities for all, resource constraints and lack of knowledge and skills can overwhelm the capability of government and non-government agencies, institutions and teachers to provide the required levels of education and training by conventional means. More and more providers are recognising that open, distance and online means of delivery have an important role to play both in providing formal schooling and tertiary education and informal and nonformal education and training for the countless millions wishing to upgrade their skills, knowledge and competences at anytime, anywhere at their own pace, and thus making the lifelong learning for all agenda a reality. This book series examines ways in which open and distance education can empower and enable individuals, groups and even entire communities to develop the knowledge and skills necessary for life and work in the 21st century, help to reduce poverty and inequality, achieve independent and sustainable development and meet the demands of the 21st century knowledge economies and open societies.

The books in this series are designed for all policy-makers, planners, managers, teachers and trainers, researchers, and students who are involved in or interested in applying open, distance and e-learning methods and technologies in informal and nonformal lifelong learning; schooling; technical and vocational education and training; higher education; workplace training and professional development; community development and international aid programmes; and serving the needs of minority groups, the disabled and other disadvantaged persons. They combine an up-to-date overview of theories, issues, core concepts and/or key literature in a particular field with case studies and practical advice in ways that will meet the needs of busy practitioners and researchers. They address such issues as access and equity, distance teaching and learning, learner support and guidance, costing, technology, assessment and learning analytics, quality assurance and evaluating outputs, outcomes and impacts, cultural factors, learning pathways and credit banking, accreditation, leadership, management, policy-making, and professional development for organisational renewal and change.

Researchers interested in authoring or editing a book for this series are invited to contact the Series Publishing Editor: alice.xie@springernature.com

All proposals will be sent out for external double-blind review. Review reports will be shared with proposers and their revisions will be further taken into consideration. The completed manuscript will be reviewed by the Series Editors and editorial advisors to ensure the quality of the book and also seek external review in order to ensure quality before formal publication.

Abstracted/Indexed in:

Scopus

Dianne Forbes · Nicola Daly · Liang Li

Designing Discussion for Online and Blended Courses

A Forum for Learning in Higher Education

Dianne Forbes
Division of Education
University of Waikato
Hamilton, New Zealand

Nicola Daly
Division of Education
University of Waikato
Hamilton, New Zealand

Liang Li
School of Arts and Education
University of Waikato
Hamilton, New Zealand

ISSN 2211-1921 ISSN 2211-193X (electronic)
SpringerBriefs in Education
ISSN 2509-4335 ISSN 2509-4343 (electronic)
SpringerBriefs in Open and Distance Education
ISBN 978-981-97-6195-1 ISBN 978-981-97-6196-8 (eBook)
https://doi.org/10.1007/978-981-97-6196-8

© The Editor(s) (if applicable) and The Author(s), under exclusive license to Springer Nature Singapore Pte Ltd. 2024

This work is subject to copyright. All rights are solely and exclusively licensed by the Publisher, whether the whole or part of the material is concerned, specifically the rights of translation, reprinting, reuse of illustrations, recitation, broadcasting, reproduction on microfilms or in any other physical way, and transmission or information storage and retrieval, electronic adaptation, computer software, or by similar or dissimilar methodology now known or hereafter developed.
The use of general descriptive names, registered names, trademarks, service marks, etc. in this publication does not imply, even in the absence of a specific statement, that such names are exempt from the relevant protective laws and regulations and therefore free for general use.
The publisher, the authors and the editors are safe to assume that the advice and information in this book are believed to be true and accurate at the date of publication. Neither the publisher nor the authors or the editors give a warranty, expressed or implied, with respect to the material contained herein or for any errors or omissions that may have been made. The publisher remains neutral with regard to jurisdictional claims in published maps and institutional affiliations.

This Springer imprint is published by the registered company Springer Nature Singapore Pte Ltd.
The registered company address is: 152 Beach Road, #21-01/04 Gateway East, Singapore 189721, Singapore

If disposing of this product, please recycle the paper.

Acknowledgements

We would like to acknowledge the contribution of Anna Juby, Research Assistant Extraordinaire, who helped with literature searches and gathering of anecdotes from online learners. This research assistance was funded by the University of Waikato, Division of Education Strategic Research Fund. We also want to acknowledge the many students who contributed to our research and teaching adventures.

Contents

1 Introduction—The Place of Online Discussion in Higher Education 1
   1.1 Learning Through Discussion: Dialogic Education and the Dialogic Space 4
   1.2 What Is Different About Discussions in Online Learning Environments? 5
   1.3 Is AOD Still Relevant? 5
   1.4 Advantages and Possibilities 6
   1.5 Actualising Affordances: Is There a Gap Between Actual and Potential AOD? 8
   References 11

2 Designing for Diversity 13
   2.1 Level of Study and Geographic Location 15
   2.2 Student Heterogeneity 16
   2.3 Return to Vignette 20
   2.4 Takeaway Tips 20
   References 22

3 Effective Learning Through Online Discussion—Enhancing Student Strategies and Experience 25
   3.1 Understand the Purpose of Discussion 26
   3.2 Develop Fluency in the Language of Discussion 27
   3.3 Manage Time and Self 29
   3.4 Add Value to the Discussion 30
   3.5 Actively Seek Feedback 31
   3.6 Take Safe Risks 32
   3.7 Challenge Politely 32
   3.8 What You Are Expected to Do in Discussion 33
   3.9 What You Should Avoid Doing—According to Feedback from Students 33

	3.10	What to Expect from Your Teachers in Our Online Discussions	34
	3.11	Scenario… Some Time Later	35
	References		35

4 Effective Teaching Through Online Discussion—Enhancing Pedagogy and Practice ... 37

- 4.1 Discussion Starter ... 38
  - 4.1.1 Discussion Topic ... 38
  - 4.1.2 Discussion Type ... 39
- 4.2 Discussion Intervention ... 41
  - 4.2.1 Maintaining Momentum with the use of Questions ... 41
  - 4.2.2 Acknowledging Students' Contributions ... 42
  - 4.2.3 Correcting Students' Posts ... 42
  - 4.2.4 Sharing New Information Including Resources, Experiences, and Opinions ... 43
  - 4.2.5 Summarising Key Points During the Discussion ... 43
  - 4.2.6 Modelling and Providing Guidance for Discussion ... 43
- 4.3 Discussion Conclusion ... 44
- 4.4 Variables Contributing to the Success of Online Discussion ... 44
  - 4.4.1 Group Size ... 45
  - 4.4.2 Frequency of Teacher Posts ... 46
  - 4.4.3 Teacher Workload ... 47
- 4.5 Return to Vignette ... 48
- 4.6 Takeaway Tips ... 48
- References ... 49

5 Assessment Issues and Practices ... 51

- 5.1 Learning and Assessment ... 52
- 5.2 Grading for Attendance and Participation ... 53
- 5.3 Assessment for Summative Purposes ... 55
- 5.4 Formative—Summative Tensions ... 57
- 5.5 Takeaway Tips ... 59
- References ... 59

6 Innovative Practices in Online Discussion ... 61

- 6.1 Content of Online Discussion ... 61
- 6.2 Involvement of Discussion Participants ... 64
  - 6.2.1 Student Roles ... 64
  - 6.2.2 Guest Lecturers and Stakeholders ... 67
- 6.3 Use of Diverse Tools ... 68
- 6.4 Return to Vignette ... 71
- 6.5 Takeaway Tips ... 71
- References ... 72

7 The Future of Online Discussion ... 75

- 7.1 Ideas for Future Directions ... 77
- References ... 78

Chapter 1
Introduction—The Place of Online Discussion in Higher Education

Abstract This introductory chapter commences with stories of the authors' first experiences with Asynchronous Online Discussion (AOD), revisiting the roots of our interest in this teaching and learning approach. We explore what happens when discussion is effective and engaging, in contrast to when it simply does not work. We foreground the goals of this book, explaining our intent to support teaching and learning through online discussion in tertiary education. Links to open, distance, and digital learning are acknowledged, along with dialogic education. The distinctiveness of discussion in online contexts is outlined, with the unique affordances of AOD. Finally, the structure of the book is introduced to orientate the reader to the chapters ahead.

Dianne's story: When I began teaching online in 2002, I was immediately captivated by the potential of asynchronous online discussion (AOD). It seemed to me that this was where deep learning can occur in an online class. I discovered I was hooked when I found myself checking online discussions frequently, losing all sense of time as I engaged in reading and responding to students' postings. I found myself thinking about discussion when away from the computer, and I would return to drop new ideas and questions into the discussion at the first available opportunity. These wonderings led me to experiment with and research asynchronous online discussion from a range of perspectives, including how guidelines for online discussion can be negotiated (Forbes, 2015), the ways teachers and students misunderstand each other in discussion (Forbes & Gedera, 2019), and students' expectations of peers in discussion (Forbes, 2022).

Liang's story: My teaching career started in 2002 at an open university, where I was fascinated by the diverse range of online teaching tools and their capabilities. What excited me the most was the opportunity to incorporate online discussion into my teaching approach, as I believe it provides a valuable space for student voices to be heard (Li, 2011; Li et al., 2012). To me, teaching begins with meeting my students where they are, addresses what they need and want, and expands through the exchange of knowledge between teachers and students.

Nicola's story: I started teaching online in 2003 for an academic writing class, and I remember feeling very overwhelmed by the new approach to teaching, but after a short time I could see the advantage of giving students quite individual attention, and the power of students learning from each other in discussions. When I began teaching a Masters paper with a colleague, we noted the ways in which our students were carefully writing their contributions to attend to the feelings of their classmates. This pricked my ears up as a sociolinguist where we refer to a theory of politeness (Brown & Levinson, 1987). My colleague and I enjoyed and found illuminating an analysis of samples of interactions using this theory (Locke & Daly, 2007).

Over time, each of us began to think of asynchronous online discussions as places and processes of deep learning and the heart of our classes. Purely subjectively, the online interaction with students has been both supportive and challenging, as students shared breakthroughs in understanding, along with their own struggles to understand. Within online classes we have used discussion in flexible and innovative ways, designing it to be relevant to wider study contexts. For example, we included a range of prompts and discussion starters, and involved external guests with specialist expertise. We noticed quality learning-oriented feedback through online discussions when students reassured each other that they were 'on the right track', or challenged each other's views and assumptions, offering new perspectives, and registering when they had changed their minds or arrived at new understandings.

This experience of discussion is ongoing. The best discussions involve formative interaction, productive argumentation, higher order thinking, and deep reciprocal learning. Participants actively build new knowledge and shared meanings and understandings by interacting, collaborating, contributing to, learning from and influencing the learning of others. There is a special place for student voice and student leadership.

Not all discussions achieve deep learning, however. There are times when discussions may be flat and uninspiring. On these occasions, participants seem to be merely going through the motions, if indeed they participate at all. Some discussions 'work' and others do not.

Students are increasingly called upon to contribute to an online discussion forum as part of flexible approaches to coursework in higher education. But just how exciting can online discussion in a university, college, or polytechnic course be? Effective discussion functions as a tutorial that weaves literature and life experience into a conversation or debate, where students and teachers build ideas through dialogue.

Based upon decades of online teaching experience, research in the field and networking with students and colleagues, this book brings together a set of understandings about the place and potential of online discussion in higher education. The goal of this book is to support teaching and learning through online discussion in tertiary education contexts such as universities, colleges, and polytechnics. There is an explicit focus on the very popular asynchronous discussion tools and methods, with attention to diversity and key principles for successful learning-oriented discussion. The book tackles the difficulties commonly experienced by students learning through online discussion. Advice for new online learners is offered in a practical and accessible way. A parallel focus looks at challenges faced by tertiary teachers implementing online discussion, outlining common concerns and productive solutions to enhance the effectiveness and manageability of online discussions for teachers. Assessment issues related to online discussion are considered. The book concludes with innovative ideas for practical application to invigorate teaching and learning through online discussion.

There is a very specific focus on online discussion rather than on a wider range of activities and interactive opportunities in online classes. The goal here is to focus on one low-tech set of teaching approaches in a powerful way. The style is succinct and accessible, with practical ideas and suggestions for transferability to a range of contexts. Importantly, there is specific attention to student and staff perspectives derived from research and incorporating both undergraduate and postgraduate levels. The book attends to what students expect from peers, which is a rare angle to consider, and challenges the teacher-centric tendency of some texts. Instead, this book includes a chapter that speaks directly to students rather than limiting itself to addressing teachers about how to help students. The book draws upon student voice and agency by relating the perspectives of students who have experienced online learning. Fundamentally, the text is underpinned by an awareness of how participants experience online discussion.

This work is likely to be useful to tertiary teachers who are teaching online as part of blended or online classes, employing online discussion. It is intended to be useful for those who are starting out with online teaching/discussion, and for those who are more advanced users seeking new ideas to refresh their practice. This will include lecturers and tutors at universities, colleges, polytechnics and private training organisations, across a wide range of disciplines and countries.

The chapter on suggestions for students could be shared with senior tertiary students, including those embarking on postgraduate study via online classes, as they learn to engage with online discussion. It is likely the staff in tertiary education settings could make the text or chapter three available to the students they work with.

Online learning is increasingly employed to enable flexibility for students and teachers, beyond the constraints of time and place. Early 2020 saw a call for universities worldwide to provide more online courses than ever before, due to COVID-19 and associated restrictions on travel for international students. In the longer term, the future of online learning is assured as environmental concerns reduce the desirability of travel, and as students demand more flexibility to select courses from a range of international providers, and to fit study around career and family lifestyles. In pursuit of flexible, sustainable learning opportunities, we reassert the value of online discussion, to augment the synchronous, video-based methods that dominated the COVID-19 crisis. Simply put, there is more to learning than Zoom conferencing. All online courses are not created equal, and quality of instruction and student experience is variable. It is not a simple matter to generate vibrant and purposeful online discussion in pursuit of learning. This book contributes to the enhancement of quality online interaction, and optimal student engagement.

This book builds upon a wealth of scholarship in the field of Open, Distance and Digital Education (ODDE, Zawacki-Richter & Jung, 2023). We use the terms online and blended learning to indicate that online discussion can augment teaching and learning practices in both fully online courses, and courses with an on-campus component. In reality, students learn across contexts, and seldom is the opportunity for learning anchored firmly in one space, whether physical or virtual. We acknowledge the roots of our practices in open and distance education (ODE), and the evolution to ODDE.

In relation to terminology, we have decided to use the term "teacher" to refer to the instructor or staff member leading the online discussion. In a tertiary context, this role is sometimes referred to by various terms, including professor, lecturer, tutor, or moderator. As each of these is a teaching role, we have elected to refer to the teacher for consistency.

1.1 Learning Through Discussion: Dialogic Education and the Dialogic Space

The idea and practice of learning through discussion is not new. There is a long history of using discussion as a teaching and learning tool generally. Discussion is a tutorial, an opportunity for shared enquiry, and a knowledge-building process. This was the case when Socrates discussed philosophy on the Agora, and it has been the case throughout human and educational history. From Socratic roots has emerged dialogic education, the essence of which is described by Wegerif (2023) in his blog as "drawing students into dialogue, asking them questions, getting them to ask questions in turn and having as your goal not just knowing about stuff but being able to ask better questions about stuff."

Whether it is oral or in the form of AOD, dialogic education is where learning occurs through problematising, posing critical questions, and exploring alternatives that lead to changes in perspective and an expansion of awareness. Insights stem from dialogues that open up new possibilities, and enable participants to "engage critically, creatively, empathetically and productively in dialogue" (Wegerif, 2023).

Online discussion is a form of dialogic education because at a basic level, teaching and learning takes the form of interaction via open ended dialogue. A more technical view of dialogic, according to earlier work by Wegerif (2018), and with reference to Bakhtin (1984) is that any single utterance (comment or post) does not make sense when viewed independently of the wider discussion including previous and subsequent contributions to the forum. As opposed to being 'monologic' with just one voice, truth or meaning, dialogic implies a multiplicity of perspectives and a discussion that promotes ongoing reflection where knowledge continues to evolve. More recently, Wegerif and Major (2024) have referred to this epistemological definition of dialogic education as "how we construct meaning from a play of voices" (p. 12), building upon the Dialogic Teaching approach developed by Alexander (2020). The intention of AOD is to turn the online discussion forum into a dialogic space. That is, a shared space where ideas merge and clash with other ideas to stimulate the emergence of new ideas (Wegerif, 2018). As Wegerif (2018) argues, it follows from this dialogic understanding of knowledge that it is more important to teach students how to construct knowledge with others and to participate in ongoing dialogues than it is to teach a body of existing knowledge. Furthermore, "engagement in dialogue is a way to change ourselves and to change our reality" (Wegerif & Major, 2024, p.12).

1.2 What Is Different About Discussions in Online Learning Environments?

There is general agreement on the differences between synchronous or in-person discussions, and asynchronous online discussions. Overall, the most significant differences relate to timing of communication and feedback.

Synchronous discussions happen in real-time, so there needs to be an agreed upon meeting time for all participants. The benefits of the simultaneous conversation are that participants are more obviously present, able to see, hear, and respond to each other, which can make for more dynamic exchanges due to immediacy. Decisions might be made more quickly if information sharing and negotiation is not spread over a longer period. On the other hand, the necessity of being present at the same time hinders flexibility across schedules and time zones and reduces reflection time. Immediacy, and the sometimes inherent haste involved in synchronous discussions are not always related to quality or depth.

Verbal communication is the norm in synchronous, face-to-face discussion, accompanied by cues like tone of voice, facial expressions and body language, as well as physical presence. This can assist clarity in communication as rich meaning is conveyed via these multiple social cues, and instant clarification can be achieved without the delay often experienced in AOD. Despite these affordances of verbal communication, it is important to note that there are also some inherent problems with face-to-face discussions (e.g., student engagement, dominance by some students, etc.). If this book is read with AOD primarily in mind, it is possible to transfer lessons from one discussion format to another.

1.3 Is AOD Still Relevant?

Asynchronous online discussions (AOD) are formally constituted, topic-centred conversations established in a specific learning environment, using a web-based bulletin or message board (Locke & Daly, 2007). The 'asynchronous' character of the discussion means that it occurs over time, with participants 'posting' messages to discussion over a period of hours or days. Communication occurs intermittently, anytime, and often at irregular intervals. Participants need not be present in the discussion simultaneously.

Asynchronous online discussion contrasts with synchronous or 'real-time' discussion, which depends on every participant being available at the same time, as in a face-to-face or Zoom conversation. While synchronicity provides a more immediate connection between people and is arguably useful in promoting social interaction, evidence suggests that synchronous online discussion tends to remain at the level of social bond formation, rather than progressing to meaningful learning (Locke, 2007).

On the other hand, research suggests that asynchronous online discussion is suited to task-oriented communication (Locke, 2007). It enables time for reflection, fostering deeper learning than synchronous discussion (Bates, 2005). By allowing participants time to compose messages, AOD may also enable more equitable and equally distributed participation (Locke, 2007).

We contend that AOD is still relevant notwithstanding the advent of new technologies that make synchronous discussion and multimedia approaches easier. Even with the growing use of social media for informal learning, and alongside the availability of Massive Open Online Courses (MOOCs), AOD is still widely used within formal educational contexts and there are still unanswered questions about how to generate effective discussion to precipitate deep learning. There are also distinct advantages in AOD.

1.4 Advantages and Possibilities

Four key AOD advantages include that:

- No one is left out or silenced—*inclusivity and equality of contribution;*
- Class time is extended—*flexibility and student choice;*
- The writing process is valued—*articulation of thinking* via *persistent text;*
- Reflection and depth are promoted—*deep learning and conceptual understanding.*

Taking each of these four advantages in turn, there is ample support in the literature for each, reinforcing AOD's educational benefits.

Inclusivity

According to the literature, AOD can promote equality of speaking time (Conrad & Donaldson, 2004). This is because the forum arrangement means that participants can talk concurrently without fear of interruption (Hewitt, 2005). Hewitt (2005) also points out that there are often higher levels of peer discourse in AOD, and in Clegg and Heap's (2006) view, this opportunity for student-to-student interaction "means that online discussions are often the glue that binds a group of students together to become a collaborative learning community" (p. 1). Every participant can have a voice.

Flexibility

The fact that AOD is neither time nor place-bound is a key advantage for flexible learning, and one that proponents of synchronous media risk in their orientation to the here and now. AOD affords convenience and accessibility, as learners choose

1.4 Advantages and Possibilities

the time and place to contribute. This choice is deemed by many to be liberating, as asynchronous duration effects free participants from "the tyranny of time" (Locke & Daly, 2007, p. 122), or by supplementing class time. Indeed, the most oft-cited benefit of AOD is 'time to think' (Guiller et al., 2008; Locke, 2007; Seddon et al., 2010). By affording time to think, the literature on AOD suggests that "Asynchronous, as opposed to synchronous, responses allow students to think through what they post, thus reducing the potential for unexamined, disrespectful, or ill-informed responses" (Fauske & Wade, 2003, p. 145). Thus, "flexibility also refers to the fact that discussion forums allow students to be flexible in their thinking. They are given time to think out structured and more in-depth responses" (Ferdig & Roehler, 2003, p. 121).

Textual communication

The fact that engaging in AOD involves reading and writing in turn affords the metalinguistic and meta-analytic advantages of print. So, learners can share thoughts and ideas informally, but can also review these, and develop habits of "careful thinking" (Ferdig & Roehler, 2003, p. 125). Garrison and Anderson (2003) argue that writing has advantages over speech for critical discourse and reflection because a persistent record is maintained. The persistent textual idea is also championed by other researchers (Haythornthwaite & Andrews, 2011). The availability of such a persistent record means that learners are more likely to be more attentive to others' views, more systematic and more exploratory. Being able to weave or synthesise ideas is enhanced because all contributions are preserved (Salmon, 2000). Writing is useful as both process and product of rigorous critical thinking, argumentation, and reflection (Garrison & Anderson, 2003; Guiller et al, 2008; Hew, Cheung & Ng, 2010).

Deep learning

Both the asynchronicity of time and the written communication format present advantages for thinking, affording thoughtful responses (Guiller et al, 2008). Having more time to think and reflect can lead to enhanced critical thinking, and to overall greater depth. Since some of this time could be spent consulting research sources, this could potentially "give rise to an increase in the use of formal, research-based evidence and the quality of critical thinking" (Guiller et al, 2008, p. 188). AOD is positively related to creative and critical thinking because participants "spend time formulating their own ideas about course concepts" (Arend, 2007, p. 14). In turn, participants question their own assumptions and perspectives and challenge those put forward by other participants (Fauske & Wade, 2003). Because of this, Conrad and Donaldson (2004) say "depth of thought is likely to be greater in a reflective online discussion than in a reactive classroom-based discussion" (p. 20).

The above four aspects (inclusivity, flexibility, textual communication and deep learning) are affordances of AOD, potentially supporting:
- Equality of contribution;
- Student choice and flexible use of time;
- Articulation via text, and the ability to revisit and synthesise persistent text;

- Thinking, reflection and depth in responses and therefore conceptual understanding.

However, as Haythornthwaite and Andrews (2011) remind us, affordances are what the media allow or make possible. Affordances such as the advantages listed above are opportunities and potential benefits but may not always be realised in practice. After all, even though "features and communicative possibilities are available does not mean they are necessarily used. This is the paradox of affordances: they are possibilities, not uses" (Haythornthwaite & Andrews, 2011, p. 67). Thus, there can be gaps between the potential and actual use of AOD for learning.

1.5 Actualising Affordances: Is There a Gap Between Actual and Potential AOD?

It is important to probe what asynchronous online discussion looks like when it is effective because effectiveness is not assured. Despite the potential affordances described above, online discussion can be dull, tedious, lacking in collaboration, frustrating for participants, and devoid of connection, emotion, disagreement or humour. Some 'discussions' are no more than a series of monologues or mini-essays, without the spirit of genuine dialogue.

For example, Bishop (2002) offers a telling critique of online discussion:

> Although asynchronous discussion is supposed to be a benefit of online learning, I found it tedious. Delays of hours or even days between postings killed their spark. Few people contradicted each other and even fewer made jokes. Unable to see each other's body language, and perhaps concerned about surveillance, students chose their words too carefully (p. 234).

In a similar vein, Thomas' (2002) critique of online discussion considers AOD to be incoherent. For Thomas (2002), this student's quote captures the essence of AOD:

> In [face-to-face] tutorials the discussion is much more alive and direct. My ideas can be changed, influenced and appreciated in a more integrated environment. The online discussion forum felt too much like monologue vs. monologue. It needs to be a discussion (p. 261).

It is apparent that both Bishop (2002) and Thomas's (2002) student have experienced AOD as lacking in energy and largely devoid of interpersonal or intellectual connection, most likely culminating in a frustrating and unsatisfactory experience. These insights into participants' personal lived experiences of online discussion lead us to ponder: What factors kill the spark of online discussion, rendering it tedious? Conversely, what can make discussion powerful and stimulating for participants?

Alongside the different experiences of AOD, researchers offer a host of explanations for the failure of discussion to realise its potential. For the most part, these explanations tend to revolve around expectations, preparation of students, rewards and modelling of participation. For example, according to Brookfield and Preskill (2005) discussion doesn't work when teachers have unrealistic expectations and where students are ill-prepared. Similarly, LaPointe (2007) and Dennen and Wieland

(2007) suggest that discussion falls short of aspirations when students are unsure of how to contribute. In addition, the literature suggests that the potential of AOD is not always met due to lack of motivation or when rewards are not evident (Brookfield & Preskill, 2005; Dennen & Wieland, 2007). Accordingly, lack of participation, or low-level participation, is frequently mentioned in the literature (Brookfield & Preskill, 2005; Dennen & Wieland, 2007; Hew et al, 2010). A key issue then, is "student involvement with discussion forums" (Ferdig & Roehler, 2003, p. 125). There is agreement that there is a crucial distinction between the affordance or opportunity offered by the technology, and the extent to which it is realised through actual social interaction among people.

Overall, the literature suggests that there is a gap between the potential and actual use of AOD when teachers and students fail to exploit the potential for dialogue and deep learning, when participants' experiences fall short of their expectations, when expectations are unclear, motivation is lacking, and participation is low or characterised by surface exchanges. This is in stark contrast to the potential AOD affords for active, deep learning. Nevertheless, as Brookfield and Preskill (2005) point out, "Never being able to get it completely right doesn't mean that we can't get better at creating the conditions under which good discussion is more likely to occur" (p. 41).

With this in mind, what are the conditions under which good discussion is more likely to occur? And what is already known about pedagogy that works with respect to AOD? Moving forward, we examine the pedagogical consensus, provide key guidelines, and suggest creative approaches to online discussion for students and teachers. We explore the need for participants in AOD to establish expectations for purposeful communication; maintain a presence for learning premised on formative interaction; and to work together in ways conducive to community and student leadership in pursuit of deep learning.

Each chapter follows a basic structure:

- An introductory scenario to set the scene
- An overview of common problems experienced
- Argument and evidence from research
- Commentary on diversity and variations on the theme
- Some advice from practitioners
- A chapter summary, with key takeaway messages

Chapter 2: Designing for diversity

This chapter highlights the importance of community in online classes, with links to the Community of Inquiry model (Garrison, Anderson & Archer, 2000). The potential for AOD in diverse settings with diverse students is explored, as sites for collaborative learning and reflective thinking. Challenges of online communication are acknowledged, with suggestions for compensating strategies. Diversity is explored in terms of geographic location, level of study, and student heterogeneity. AOD is analysed in relation to prominent frameworks of universal design for learning, and culturally responsive teaching.

Chapter 3: Effective learning through online discussion—enhancing student strategies and experience

This chapter provides suggestions for students who are new to learning through online discussion. The chapter will also function as a standalone piece that could be read by students as they work to understand the rationale for discussion, and how best to contribute in order to maximise the learning opportunities offered by discussion. Much of the material underpinning suggestions for students is based upon testimony from undergraduate and postgraduate students who have shared their concerns and issues in relation to learning through online discussion. This chapter acknowledges the anxieties and doubt experienced by novices to online discussion, and advises on how to clarify expectations, incorporating advice from students who are experienced online learners. In brief, most teachers expect that students will participate, interact, reflect, widen perspectives and link to literature and professional practice. While these expectations will vary across disciplines and contexts, students are advised to ascertain what the ground rules are for discussion in their course. Specific guidelines are provided regarding the behaviours to aim for, and those to avoid, when participating in online discussion.

Chapter 4: Effective teaching through online discussion – enhancing pedagogy and practice

This chapter looks at how teachers can convene and moderate online discussions in ways that are effective for student learning and engagement; time-efficient; varied and satisfying. The chapter tackles basic organizational factors such as grouping, topics, links to class, and assignments, purpose/s, and how to guide students.

A key point of reference is acknowledgement of common concerns for teachers:

- How might I keep the online discussions interesting and varied?
- How can I ensure the students participate in each discussion?
- How often do I have to post in discussion?
- How time consuming will this be, alongside my research, administration and service commitments, as well as life outside of work?

Chapter four provides guidance on how to establish a purpose for discussion, maintain appropriate presence, promote student participation and learning, and manage time and self effectively to keep workload under control.

Chapter 5: Assessment issues and practices

This chapter outlines the formative and summative uses of online discussion, with examples of each. Assessment is often a contentious issue, not least because summative assessment can constrain students' participation and their enjoyment of discussion, inhibiting their expression of genuine views. Tensions between formative and summative assessment are explored, with a view to promoting deep learning. The practice of grading participation is critiqued. Formatively, discussion can function as interactive formative assessment, where students and teachers give and receive feedback and feedforward, in a timely fashion. Importantly, teachers are not the only source of such feedback, and peer and self-assessment can happen alongside teachers' monitoring discussions to identify and address misconceptions and to extend ideas.

Since assessment influences both how students spend their time and the type of learning taking place, the challenge is to assess in such a way as to encourage deep as opposed to surface approaches to learning. Solutions are proposed in this chapter, across a range of options and contexts.

Chapter 6: Innovative practices in online discussion

This chapter looks at creative approaches to discussion, with a focus on innovative content, ways of involving participants, and variations to online tools. We consider the integration of active and practical learning with AOD, and provide specific examples of activities used in online classes. We advocate challenging students' thinking by allocating leadership roles and eliciting fresh perspectives; inviting guests to participate; and extending the use of a range of digital tools to enrich the discussion.

Chapter 7: The future of online discussion

This chapter wraps up the various threads in the text and provides a forward-looking statement regarding future work to be done, with key messages for a range of readers.

References

Alexander, R. (2020). *A dialogic teaching companion*. Routledge.

Arend, B. D. (2007). Course assessment practices and student learning strategies in online courses. *Journal of Asynchronous Learning Networks, 11*(4), 3–17.

Bates. (Tony), A. W. (2005). *Technology, e-learning and distance education* (2nd ed.). Routledge.

Bishop, A. (2002). Come into my parlour said the spider to the fly: Critical reflections of web-based education from a student's perspective. *Distance Education, 23*(2), 231–236.

Brookfield, S., & Preskill, S. (2005). *Discussions as a way of teaching: tools and techniques for democratic classrooms* (2nd ed.). Jossey-Bass.

Brown, P., & Levinson, S. C. (1987). Politeness: Some universals in language usage (Vol. 4). Cambridge university press.

Clegg, P., & Heap, J. (2006). Facing the challenge of e-learning: Reflections on teaching evidence-based practice through online discussion groups. *Innovate, 2*(6). Avail: http://innovateonline.info/

Conrad, R., & Donaldson, J. A. (2004). *Engaging the online learner: Activities and resources for creative instruction*. Jossey-Bass.

Dennen, V. P., & Wieland, K. (2007). From interaction to intersubjectivity: Facilitating online group discourse processes. *Distance Education, 28*(3), 281–297.

Fauske, J., & Wade, S. E. (2003). Research to practice online: Conditions that foster democracy, community, and critical thinking in computer-mediated discussions. *Journal of Research on Technology in Education, 36*(2), 137–153.

Ferdig, R. E., & Roehler, L. R. (2003). Student uptake in electronic discussions: Examining online discourse in literacy preservice classrooms. *Journal of Research on Technology in Education, 26*(2), 119–136.

Forbes, D. (2015). Legacies of learning: Negotiating guidelines for online discussion. In N. Wright, & D. Forbes (Eds.), Digital smarts: enhancing learning and teaching (pp. 82–103). Hamilton, New Zealand: Wilf Malcolm Institute of Educational Research.

Forbes, D., & Gedera, D. (2019). From confounded to common ground: misunderstandings between tertiary teachers and students in online discussions. *Australasian Journal of Educational Technology, 35*(4), 13 pages. https://doi.org/10.14742/ajet.3595

Forbes, D. (2022). Student expectations of peers in academic asynchronous online discussion. *Journal of Open, Flexible and Distance Learning, 26*(1), 27–41. https://doi.org/10.61468/jofdl.v26i1.505

Garrison, D. R., & Anderson, T. (2003). *E-learning in the 21st century*. London & New York: Routledge Falmer.

Garrison, D. R., Anderson, T., & Archer, W. (2000). Critical inquiry in a text-based environment: Computer conferencing in higher education. *The Internet and Higher Education, 2*(2–3), 1–19.

Guiller, J., Durndell, A., & Ross, A. (2008). Peer interaction and critical thinking: Face-to-face or online discussion? *Learning and Instruction, 18*(2), 187–200.

Haythornthwaite, C., & Andrews, R. (2011). *E-learning theory and practice*. Sage Publications.

Hew, K. F., Cheung, W. S., & Ng, C. S. L. (2010). Student contribution in asynchronous online discussion: A review of the research and empirical exploration. *Instructional Science*, 571–606.

Hewitt, J. (2005). Toward an understanding of how threads die in asynchronous computer conferences. *Journal of the Learning Sciences, 14*(4), 567–589.

LaPointe, D. K. (2007). Pursuing interaction. In J. M. Spector (Ed.), *Finding your voice online: Stories told by experienced online educators* (pp. 83–103). Lawrence Erlbaum Associates Inc.

Li, L. (2011). 突破在线教学瓶颈促进学生社会性交互 [Enhancing online education: Social interaction strategies between students]. *中国远程教育, 21*, 47–50.

Li, L., Qiao, H., & Wang, S. (2012). 基于Moodle平台的学习者社会性交互特征研究 [Exploring different types of social interactions between learners on Moodle platforms]. *电化教育研究, 33*(7), 48–53.

Locke, T. (2007). E-learning and the reshaping of rhetorical space. In R. Andrews & C. A. Haythornthwaite (Eds.), *The Sage handbook of e-learning research* (pp. 179–201). Sage Publications.

Locke, T., & Daly, N. (2007). Towards congeniality: The place of politeness in asynchronous online discussion. *International Journal of Learning, 13*(12), 121–134.

Salmon, G. (2000). *E-Moderating: The key to teaching and learning online*. Kogan Page.

Seddon, K., Postlethwaite, K., & Lee, G. (2010). Understanding the experience of non contributory online participants (readers) in National College for School Leadership online communities. *Education and Information Technologies, 16*(4), 343–363.

Thomas, M. J. W. (2002). Learning within incoherent structures: The space of online discussion forums. *Journal of Computer Assisted Learning, 18*(3), 351–366.

Wegerif, R. (2018). A dialogic theory of teaching thinking. In Kerslake, L., & Wegerif, R. (Eds). Theory of teaching thinking, pp. 89–104, Routledge. https://doi.org/10.4324/9781315098944

Wegerif, R. (2023). Will ChatGPT turn education back to Socrates? https://www.rupertwegerif.name/blog/will-chatgpt-turn-education-back-to-socrates

Wegerif, R., & Major, L. (2024). *The theory of educational technology: Towards a dialogic foundation for design*. Routledge.

Zawacki-Richter, O., & Jung, I. (2023) (Eds.). *Handbook of open, distance and digital education*. Springer.

Chapter 2
Designing for Diversity

Abstract This chapter highlights the importance of community in online classes, with links to the Community of Inquiry model. The potential for AOD in diverse settings with diverse students is explored, as sites for collaborative learning and reflective thinking. Challenges of online communication are acknowledged, with suggestions for compensating strategies. Diversity is explored in terms of geographic location, level of study, and student heterogeneity. AOD is analysed in relation to prominent frameworks of universal design for learning, and culturally responsive teaching.

Recently Angie, while doing a floristry course online through a technical institute remarked: I saw another student's question/comment in the Q&A space talking about the best sources of information for our floristry work. I replied to her and suggested that we start with the coursework as there seems to be a lot of variation in the wider sources available (apps, sites, etc.). The tutor came in and agreed with me, and it was the best and most interaction we have had in the whole course! Usually, I just complete the readings, activities, and assignments, but I never get to talk with other participants in the course. I think we should talk more online, and I would like the feedback too.

This scenario brings up several aspects of importance in relation to the effective use of Asynchronous Online Discussions (AODs) in tertiary education. The first of these is the importance of community, specifically a Community of Inquiry. The Community of Inquiry model was developed to explain the potential of online discussions for supporting the development of higher order thinking skills (Garrison et al., 1999) and consists of three core components: social presence, cognitive presence, and teaching presence. It is discussed repeatedly and extensively in the research literature (e.g., Li & Yu, 2020; Lowenthal & Dunlap, 2020; Nolan-Grant, 2019) in relation to effective online discussion. In the scenario involving Angie and the online floristry course, Angie reports that she usually just completes her online work in isolation, but she noticed the benefits of talking to her classmate and her teacher when it happened by chance. That is, while content or cognitive presence was in place, Angie could complete her work, but she noticed and appreciated the addition of social and teaching presence. The second point of interest from this scenario is the use of AODs in floristry education. It is easy to think of AODs as being only used in more traditional print-based tertiary education, but they are being used in a range of contexts around the world with students in undergraduate and postgraduate courses. In this chapter we explore literature about how AODs are used in diverse settings with diverse students.

"Online learning communities are commonly described as offering social or emotional support as well as facilitating learning through collaboration and cooperation" (Lander, 2015, p. 108). As discussed in the previous chapter, discussion boards are tools which allow for asynchronous discussions, and the power of asynchronous online discussions has been identified as relating to the way in which it fosters collaborative learning (Ouyang & Chan, 2019), encourages participation (Osborne, Byrne, Massey & Johnstone, 2018) and the space it allows for students to reflect on ideas with the support or scaffolding of a teacher, thus promoting critical thinking (Aloni & Harrington, 2018). Indeed, students interviewed from an Australian introductory Information Technology cohort reported that participating in AOD helped them with critical thinking skills by reading different perspectives written by their peers and with developing their arguments (Klisc, McGill & Hobbs, 2017). The USA preservice teachers in a study by Hambacher et al. (2018) in a classroom management paper also reported that the asynchronous nature of online discussions allowed them "to structure their ideas and engage in reflection in a way that is not possible in face-to-face classrooms" (p. 157).

While AODs where purpose and expectations of discussions are clearly communicated appear to allow for increased participation from introverted students, they also pose the risk of students feeling isolated and experiencing misunderstandings due to the lack of nonverbal cues (Aloni & Harrington, 2018). However, there is growing recognition that participants in AOD can compensate for reduced or filtered cues with a variety of strategies (Dennen & Wieland, 2007; Garrison & Anderson, 2003; Herring, 1999; Rourke et al., 1999). Compensating strategies include using social acknowledgements, paralinguistic emphasis (such as emoticons/emojis), personal vignettes or self-disclosure (Dennen & Wieland, 2007; Garrison & Anderson, 2003). The challenge for participants in AOD is learning how to effectively use and learn from these compensating strategies. Some theorists suggest that this is tantamount to learning a new language with distinct local patterns and norms (Bregman & Haythornthwaite, 2003; Haythornthwaite & Andrews, 2011). Hambacher et al. (2018) note that "whereas in face-to-face classroom discussions it is common for some students to remain on the periphery, the online setting provides an entry point for students who do not readily speak in class" (p. 250). These affordances and challenges of AODs may vary in relation to a range of characteristics of students, including the level of their study (graduate or undergraduate), gender, language proficiency or ability, and interwoven across these are the geographic location of the participants and the subject being studied.

2.1 Level of Study and Geographic Location

While the topic of diversity has been extensively considered in relation to primary and secondary education (e.g., Bishop & Berryman, 2006; Moll et al., 1992), there has been a paucity of research specifically addressing diversity in tertiary education, specifically online learning in tertiary education. It is left to the reader to note that some studies have explored AODs in undergraduate programmes such as Peng, Han, Ouyong and Liu (2020) who tracked topics in small private online courses in a Chinese university showing that the intensity of students' attention to topics of discussion fluctuated. Asif, Vertejee and Lalani (2016) worked with 24 Pakistani undergraduate nursing students, showing that there was low online engagement and facilitator participation in online posts. In another part of the world, Murphy and Fortner (2014) worked with undergraduate technology students in the USA, comparing one online discussion group in which the tutor posted and another where there were no teacher postings, showing that while the presence of a tutor did not affect the quality of posts, it did affect participation rates negatively, that is as the teacher posted more frequently, the student posted less frequently. There is tension in the literature around this finding. A significant body of research indicates that teachers should be present, active and responsive so that they extend students' thinking (diagnose misconceptions and model critical thinking). Otherwise, students may remain in "continuous exploration mode" (Garrison et al., 2001, p. 10). Accordingly, there is support for the view that teaching presence is needed to move the discussion beyond surface exchanges, and to prompt deeper learning (Bates, 2005; Collison et al., 2000; Ferdig & Roehler, 2003). On the other side of the debate is the minimal intervention stance, warning that if teachers are too authoritative in discussion, this discourages students. There may also be a sense of surveillance because of which students feel they can't speak freely. The middle ground is a balance, where the teacher is attentive and responsive, but avoids dominating and having the final word in the discussion.

Chen and Huang (2018) explored how prestige amongst student AOD participants was explained. In a USA undergraduate course in technology, ethics and society, Chen and Huang (2018) defined 'high prestige' students as those who had more incoming communication, a higher chance of having their post responded to, and stronger ties (interactions) with other students. They found that it was not post length, the use of questions or the readability of the posts which characterised the high prestige group of students, but the timeliness of the high prestige students' posts. The high prestige students posted earlier than the group of students with less prestige, thus allowing more time for students to respond. The focus of the research involving AODs being used by undergraduate students comes out of a range of geographic locations and focuses on different aspects of the efficacy of online discussions, but none of the findings seem strikingly different in relation to their location or subject material.

Nor does it seem that research concerning the use of AODs in postgraduate settings provides findings of a different kind to those with undergraduate students. Brierton et al. (2016) worked with the online discussions in a Master's degree Agricultural extension programme comparing evidence in AOD posts of higher order thinking skills in synchronous and asynchronous online discussion. Using an assessment tool of cognitive behaviour based on Blooms' taxonomy, they showed a statistically significant difference between the cognitive level evident in asynchronous posts compared with synchronous posts. Nolan-Grant (2019) in the United Kingdom used the Community of Inquiry framework to explore online presence of students and tutors in a postgraduate 3 week module of an online course, showing that there was increased participation by both students and tutors (number of posts made and videos watched) when the Community of Inquiry components of social, cognitive and teaching presence were related. McPhee (2015) explored the use of AODs with Australian music teachers over a 7-month period, showing that while the AOD provided a space in which students could share their real-world strategies for music teaching, creating "a repository of strategies that teachers could draw from, return to, and reflect upon" (p. 116). In a Spanish postgraduate online course concerning the development of thinking in adolescence, Martinez and Alvarez Valdinia (2016) showed that the use of a graphical tool in the online discussions did not enhance student learning. Work with students in a USA educational leadership programme over a 15-week semester by Lowenthal and Dunlap (2020) explored how to establish social presence in online discussions, noting that while the Community of Inquiry framework in undoubtedly central to effective online discussions, it does not provide guidance on how to design courses or facilitate discussion in order to achieve this. They note that social presence is enhanced by smaller discussion groups, establishment of relationships prior to online discussions, and particular instructional tasks for students working in pairs, project groups or reading groups.

Thus, while there is a wealth of research about understanding and enhancing effective online discussions in both undergraduate and postgraduate tertiary settings, there does not seem to have been specific comparisons between these two contexts; certainly, research findings suggest that central to both settings is the importance of social presence, creating the context for community of inquiry through discussion design and instructions. Research appears to have been published from many geographic settings from around the world, again showing no obvious or thematic differences in relation to geographic differences.

2.2 Student Heterogeneity

Work on other aspects of diversity has been more specifically addressed, if somewhat haphazardly. O'Brien and Kerma (2019) explored how student heterogeneity affected the use of resources amongst first year Bachelor of Commerce students in an Australian university, finding that while Business students attended or watched lectures, economics students downloaded lecture notes. Perhaps even more interesting, was the finding that female students and older students used digital resources more than lecture attendance in their study practice. O'Brien and Kerma (2019) note that to their knowledge this is the only research showing this gender difference but fail to suggest the most obvious reason for this, that women and older students often perform many other roles within a family which may mean that face-to-face attendance is not possible.

Work by Lander (2014, 2015) exploring the linguistic strategies used with Australian health professionals in online learning situations has shown the potential influence of language practices on the marginalisation of some groups in online discussions. Lander notes, for example, that some of the affective, cohesive and interactive strategies used by teachers in moderated discussions may serve to support the 'invisible curriculum' identified by Bernstein (2000), inadvertently contributing to the marginalisation of some groups. Lander advises the use of self-introduction, self-disclosure and overt empathy to build community, warning against negative judgement and the pitfalls of humour which is usually culturally located. Further analysis showed that participants were often unsure of how spoken-like or written-like their posting language should be. In an English-medium context, those participants who used English as an additional language and those with less professional experience often struggled to write appropriate texts, while native speakers and those with extensive professional experience wrote their posts with more confidence. We note that if both the teachers and students are fluent in language(s) other than the dominant language of instruction, these language(s) can be utilised in online discussions in conjunction with or in lieu of the dominant language of instruction to facilitate more effective communication.

Dahstrom-Hakki, Alstad and Banerjee (2020) note that "online learning is particularly challenging for students with disabilities because of high demands on executive function skills such as response inhibition and problem solving" (p.150). Their work with 105 students with high incidence disabilities (e.g. learning disabilities, ADHD and ASD) in a private USA university showed that while these students preferred synchronous discussion, their performance in relation to conceptual understanding was improved following asynchronous discussions. They suggest that the speed needed for synchronous discussions may have impeded cognitive processing and social dynamics for this cohort of students.

In an excellent review of literature to summarise the affordances and challenges of AOD, Aloni and Harrington (2018) conclude that the benefits of AOD include students being able to work at their own pace, an extension of classroom discussion beyond the classroom, the facilitation of peer learning, the involvement of more introverted or socially marginalised students, and the facilitation of critical thinking. The challenges include the lack of student participation when the purpose and expectations of the discussions are unclear or if students experience low self-confidence or technical difficulties. Other challenges include students feeling disconnected or experiencing misunderstanding due to the lack of nonverbal cues, as well as teachers knowing how to pitch the level of their involvement in online discussions.

It is interesting to consider these ideas in light of a recent document concerning culturally responsive teaching in tertiary settings. The recently released Ngā Hau e whā o Tāwhirimātea. Culturally Responsive Teaching and Learning for the Tertiary Sector (Rātima et al., 2022) is a range of suggestions from research and case studies with pedagogical examples to show what being culturally responsive in a tertiary setting might look like. Key Māori values are identified, including Manaakitanga (ethic of care), Kotahitanga (working together), Whanaungatanga (recognising relationships) and Rangatiratanga (recognising expertise) to describe the range of ways in which tertiary educators in Aotearoa New Zealand can be culturally responsive. All four areas revolve around Oranga (health and wellbeing) (see Fig. 2.1). In the remainder of this chapter, we will consider how the practices shown in the research to be effective in AOD fit within a culturally responsive framework.

Firstly Manaakitanga, translated as an ethic of care which models respect for diversity, creating a sense of belonging through representation. When Manaakitanga is at play in a culturally diverse tertiary context, classroom learning draws on cultural and linguistic differences and similarities. Research by Lander (2014; 2015) suggests that without linguistic awareness it is possible that the prompts and feedback used by online teachers in tertiary AODs may maintain the linguistic hegemony of the face-to-face classroom, potentially disadvantaging participants who use the medium of instruction as an additional language by the way in which prompts and feedback are indirectly phrased. The corollary of this is the time afforded by AODs does allow those less confident with their academic language use to craft and refine their post before contributing it to the online discussion. Thus, there is potential with increased awareness of language use which may seem opaque to additional language users, that AODs offer affordances which can contribute to Manaakitanga in an online learning

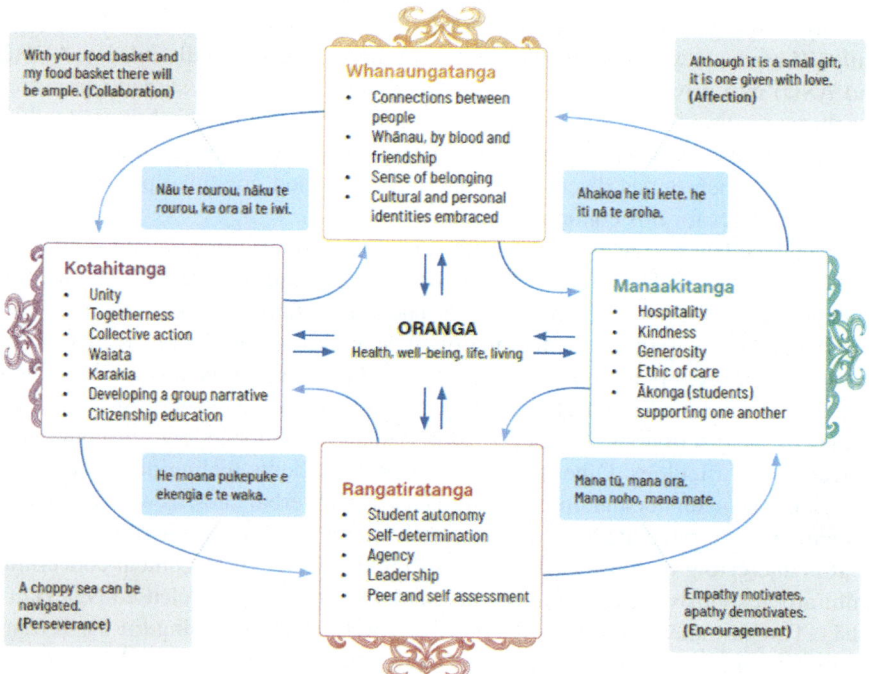

Fig. 2.1 Ngā Hau e Whā o Tāwhirimātea (Rātima et al., 2022, p. 15)

environment. If in addition to this awareness of and inclusiveness towards language use, students are encouraged to critique the choices of examples and languages used in AODs and are encouraged to share their cultural practices; if they see their peers' culture(s) represented in examples shared and resources used, Manaakitanga can be further enhanced. The modelling of kindness in responses to online contributions and encouragement for akonga (students) to support one another in online discussions by respectfully building on the ideas and posts contributed before them will also contribute to culturally responsive digital learning spaces. Indeed, research concerning AODs in an online postgraduate arts and language course involving students from New Zealand and China, identified the ways in which students used positive politeness strategies to negotiate their online discussions including inclusive group forms of address, and intensification of interest in what classmates contribute and the acknowledgement of common ground (Locke & Daly, 2007).

The second of the values represented in Rātima et al.'s (2022) model of culturally responsive is Kotahitanga, commonly translated into English as Unity, or building group understanding through shared observations. This ties in strongly with the idea of a Community of Inquiry (Lander et al., 2016) often referenced as the key to effective meaning making in social constructivism. When online posting in an AOD is framed as a collaborative activity in which participants are encouraged to build on the contributions of their peers, kotahitanga is at work, contributing to the cultural responsiveness of the online community. The mutual respect evident in the positive politeness strategies used by postgraduate arts and language students from New Zealand and China (Locke & Daly, 2007), is an example of kotahitanga. If further emphasis on the group work done in AODs can be enhanced, it is likely that this aspect of cultural responsiveness will also be further enhanced. This may include ensuring that the online discussions are not dominated by the lecturer's voice, and that student-led discussions are encouraged by giving students particular roles to perform in online discussions (Ghadrian & Ayub, 2017; Ghardinian, Salihi & Ayub, 2018).

The third Māori value in *Ngā Hau e Whā* (Rātima, et al., 2022) is Whanaungatanga or relationships. When students in AOD contexts are asked to introduce themselves prior to AODs, and when they conduct their discussions in smaller groups which enhances the quality of the online discussions (Lowenthal & Dunlap, 2020), these practices contribute to whanaungatanga and the overall Oranga or health and wellbeing of AOD participants. Relationships can be established and maintained through AOD as students and teachers share and respond to each other. This can create a sense of belonging, collaboration, and scaffolding of learning. Feedback that acknowledges the efforts and ideas of students is an important aspect of the teacher's role, as well as the role of peers in the AOD. Because the AOD functions as a shared learning experience, it is a foundation for whanaungatanga. Importantly, students and teachers should be encouraged to share their own experiences in AOD, whether these be personal or professional experiences. Valuing participant experiences is a way of acknowledging where people come from and what they bring to the discussion. Sharing connections forms new connections.

And lastly, Rangatiratanga which is a recognition of student agency, self-determination and leadership. This can happen when students are positioned as active learners in an AOD using prompts which are open and inclusive, being asked to respond to resources with their own thoughts, interpretations and reflections to make meaning. When students are asked to link what they read and hear to their own experiences, their rangatiratanga is being recognised and respected. Students can be positioned as cultural experts by the provision of opportunities within AODs to reveal their personal cultural understandings and to share their personal experiences of cultural events. Students may be encouraged to be as active learners within AOD contexts by enabling discussion which allows students to develop personal understandings, by perhaps being encouraged to ask for explanations, clarifications and to listen and respond to experts. There is also potential for teachers to explicitly model the learner role through asking questions, responding to 'expert' information that is shared, and then stepping back to make room for students to lead as learners.

2.3 Return to Vignette

And lastly, we return to the vignette we began with when Angie commented on her experience of online discussions in an online floristry course. Here we see an example where a community of inquiry has not been set up, and where a chance interaction showed Angie the potential of what she might be missing out on in terms of whanaungatanga- relationships. When Angie's rangatiratanga was recognised by her tutor when she replied to her classmate in the AOD, she experienced a sense of enjoyment of her learning which she hadn't previously, and perhaps regret at the potential which was not being realised. And so, we see in action two of the key values of culturally responsive teaching in an online learning environment in our initial vignette. Manaakitanga is also evident in the way Angie supported another student who had originally asked the question about the best sources of information for their floristry studies. Ākonga supporting one another is a form of Manaakitanga; and Kotahitanga is present in terms of a sense of the collective, evident when Angie felt more togetherness and part of a group, rather than isolated as the result of her interaction online.

2.4 Takeaway Tips

Research on AODs has not addressed the role of diversity specifically, by comparing practice in different subject areas. However, when comparing literature from a range of geographic and disciplinary locations, effective AOD practice has more similarities than differences. We now share some tips for practitioners to consider in their own AODs.

Provide opportunities for students to

2.4 Takeaway Tips

- Share who they are with their classmates
- Build relationships with their classmates
- Draw on their own experiences
- Listen to and build on the posts of their classmates
- Experience teachers' care for them and their learning within the AOD

AODs can be designed using the principles of Universal Design for Learning (UDL) to create an inclusive and engaging learning environment for all students. UDL principles can be applied to asynchronous online discussions to ensure opportunities for learning are flexible, equitable, and intuitive (King-Sears, 2009). Accordingly, AOD can enable multiple options for representation of content, action and expression, and student engagement (CAST, 2018; Ismailov & Chiu, 2022).

Here are some tips for incorporating UDL into your AODs:

- Multiple means of presentation
    - Share content in different formats to support understanding. This can include incorporating audio, video, and visual aids such as diagrams and infographics into AOD. It also entails using clear and simple language in AOD, and ensuring jargon is explained. Students can also be encouraged to research and bring findings to the online discussion forum.
- Multiple opportunities for action and expression
    - Invite students to demonstrate their knowledge and skills in different ways—giving students the option to respond to discussion prompts in writing, audio or video recordings, or other creative formats such as infographics or digital storytelling.
- Multiple options for engagement and interaction
    - Create opportunities for students to engage with the content in different ways. This can include providing choice and autonomy in discussion topics, encouraging peer-to-peer interaction, and fostering a sense of community and collaboration among students.

By incorporating these principles into AODs, educators can create a more inclusive and accessible learning environment that supports the diverse needs and strengths of all students.

Having explored research concerning addressing diversity in AOD pedagogical practices, we note that there is a divide between teachers' intentions and students' experiences, and between teachers' and students' expectations of learning and support. For this reason, the following two chapters are devoted in turn to students, and to teachers.

References

Aloni, M., & Harrington, C. (2018). Research based practices for improving the effectiveness of asynchronous online discussion boards. *Scholarship of Teaching and Learning in Psychology, 4*(4), 271.

Bernstein, B. (2000). *Pedagogy, symbolic control and identity: Theory, research, critique* (Revised). Rowman and Littlefield.

Bishop, R., & Berryman, M. (2006). *Culture speaks: Cultural relationships and classroom learning.* Huia Publishers.

Brierton, S., Wilson, E., Kistler, M., Flowers, J., & Jones, D. (2016). A comparison of higher order thinking skills demonstrated in synchronous and asynchronous online college discussion posts. *Nacta Journal, 60*(1), 14–21.

Dahlstrom-Hakki, I., Alstad, Z., & Banerjee, M. (2020). Comparing synchronous and asynchronous online discussions for students with disabilities: The impact of social presence. *Computers and Education, 150*, 103842.

Garrison, D. R., Anderson, T., & Archer, W. (1999). Critical inquiry in a text-based environment: Computer conferencing in higher education. *The Internet and Higher Education, 2*(2–3), 87–105.

Ghadirian, H., Fauzi Mohd Ayub, A., & Salehi, K. (2018). Students' perceptions of online discussions, participation and e-moderation behaviours in peer-moderated asynchronous online discussions. *Technology, Pedagogy and Education, 27*(1), 85–100

Hambacher, E., Ginn, K., & Slater, K. (2018). Letting students lead: Preservice teachers' experiences of learning in online discussions. *Journal of Digital Learning in Teacher Education, 34*(3), 151–165.

Klisc, C., McGill, T., & Hobbs, V. (2017). Use of a post-asynchronous online discussion assessment to enhance student critical thinking. *Australasian Journal of Educational Technology, 33*(5).

Lander, J. (2014). Conversations or virtual IREs? Unpacking asynchronous online discussions using exchange structure analysis. *Linguistics and Education, 28*, 41–53.

Lander, J. (2015). Building community in online discussion: A case study of moderator strategies. *Linguistics and Education, 29*, 107–120.

Li, X., & Yu, Y. (2020). Characteristics of asynchronous online discussions in a graduate course: An exploratory study. *Information and Learning Sciences, 121*(7/8), 599–609.

Locke, T., & Daly, N. (2007). Towards congeniality: The place of politeness in asynchronous online discussion. *International Journal of Learning, 13*(12).

Lowenthal, P. R., & Dunlap, J. C. (2020). Social presence and online discussions: A mixed method investigation. *Distance Education, 41*(4), 490–514.

McPhee, E. (2015). Learning through talking: Web forum conversations as facilitation for instrumental teacher professional development. *Australian Journal of Music Education, 2*, 107–117.

Moll, L. C., Amanti, C., Neff, D., & Gonzalez, N. (1992). Funds of knowledge for teaching: Using a qualitative approach to connect homes and classrooms. *Theory into Practice, 31*(2), 132–141.

Nolan-Grant, C. R. (2019). The Community of Inquiry framework as learning design model: a case study in postgraduate online education. *Research in learning technology, 27*.

Osborne, D. M., Byrne, J. H., Massey, D. L., & Johnston, A. N. (2018). Use of online asynchronous discussion boards to engage students, enhance critical thinking, and foster staff-student/student-student collaboration: A mixed method study. *Nurse Education Today, 70*, 40–46.

Ouyang, F., & Chang, Y. H. (2019). The relationships between social participatory roles and cognitive engagement levels in online discussions. *British Journal of Educational Technology, 50*(3), 1396–1414.

Peng, X., Han, C., Ouyang, F., & Liu, Z. (2020). Topic tracking model for analyzing student-generated posts in SPOC discussion forums. *International Journal of Educational Technology in Higher Education, 17*(1), 1–22.

References

Rātima, T. M., Smith, J. P., Macfarlane, A. H., Riki, N. M., Jones, K. L., & Davies, L. K. (2022). Ngā Hau e Whā o Tāwhirimātea: Culturally responsive teaching and learning for the Tertiary Sector.

Chapter 3
Effective Learning Through Online Discussion—Enhancing Student Strategies and Experience

Abstract This chapter provides suggestions for students who are new to learning through Asynchronous Online Discussion (AOD). Much of the evidence underpinning the suggestions here is based upon testimony from undergraduate and postgraduate students who have shared their concerns and issues in relation to learning through AOD. We acknowledge the anxiety and doubt experienced by novices to online discussion, and advise on how to clarify expectations, incorporating advice from students who are experienced online learners. We provide specific guidelines for behaviours to aim for, and those to avoid, when participating in AOD.

Logging into the Learning Management System, Jamie finds the latest forum and immediately glazes over... So many threads, so many posts, what to make of all of this... The discussion has been open for four days now, but Jamie forgot about it until now.

Clicking into the discussion at random, Jamie starts to read. Some of the posts are so long! They might as well be writing an essay, thinks Jamie. Other posts are just two words: I agree. Well, that's dull, thinks Jamie, so what?! There is pressure to add a response, but Jamie thinks the topic has been covered already—what else is there to add? What if I contradict someone and they become angry? What if I look stupid? I guess I'll just repeat what has already been said, it is all pointless anyway.

As illustrated in Jamie's story, some of the biggest concerns students have about discussion include:

- A lack of understanding of the purpose of the discussion—What is the point of this anyway?
- Challenges with time/self management—I keep forgetting to go into the discussion, when I am busy with my other classes. By the time I join the discussion, I am overwhelmed by the volume of messages and feel I have nothing new to add.
- If I think of something to add to the discussion, how will I know I am on the right track? Maybe I'll look stupid, and that comment will be there forever.
- I might upset someone so I'll play it safe, but this is really boring.

Taking each of these concerns in turn, the following advice for students is supported by evidence from research and practice.

3.1 Understand the Purpose of Discussion

Online discussion functions as a tutorial; it is an opportunity for teaching and learning. The rationale for discussion is three-fold:

1. As individuals, we engage in discussion in order to learn from and with each other. Ideally, discussion should involve testing out ideas, sharing and building on other people's thinking, and gaining feedback and challenge from others' responses to our own thinking. There is very rarely one single answer to any worthwhile question. Rather, the best discussions require thinking of a higher order, where multiple answers and perspectives are possible and actively encouraged.
2. As a community, teachers and learners have a responsibility to each other to relate and respond actively and to learn together, supporting others' learning as well as our own. Students should contribute to online discussion so that they don't let group members down, and so that comments aren't ignored.
3. In society, as citizens and professionals, graduates are expected to participate in discussion with colleagues (whether face-to-face or online), and to be aware of a range of thinking, perspectives, theory, practice, and issues. Discussions in class are good preparation for the professional discussions that will be ongoing throughout our lives and careers.

Most lecturers expect that students will participate, interact, reflect, widen perspectives and link to literature and professional practice or relevant personal experience (Forbes & Gedera, 2019). While these expectations will vary across disciplines and contexts, students are advised to ascertain what the ground rules are for discussion in their course. Usually, lecturers will ensure expectations are clearly communicated via course documentation, including the rationale for discussion, learning outcomes, assessment criteria, and how the discussion fits into the course. Where students remain uncertain about the expectations for discussion, it is wise for students to directly ask the lecturer or convenor of the course. Students might ask for models and exemplars of effective discussion. Lecturers, in turn, can create or collect these exemplars with student permission, and share them in order to clarify and illustrate the expectations of effective AOD.

While it will often be the case, as noted, that lecturers will stipulate the guidelines and expectations for discussion, there may also be a more democratic approach to co-constructing guidelines with students (Forbes, 2015). Lecturers can seek students' input to generate common understandings as a foundation for learning together. Once students have participated in AOD, they will have a sense of the pros and cons, what works well or hinders their learning, and what they need from their fellow participants in dialogue (Forbes, 2022). Gathering up student suggestions is a way of tailoring discussion guidelines to each cohort and context so that expectations evolve with each class.

In a well-designed course, the topics of discussion will logically reflect the learning intentions of the course. Typically, each discussion will commence with a prompt from the lecturer in terms of a question, quotation, problem, scenario, or similar challenge for students to consider. Understanding the topic is a first step and may involve reading and exploring wider course materials, as well as undertaking independent research. Students can contribute to discussion by deconstructing the topic—clarifying key terms, rephrasing the topic in their own words, and explicitly inviting other perspectives.

When contributions to AOD are assessed, there should be a set of criteria, and good practice suggests this be shared in advance with students in order to clarify purpose, expectations, and to assist students with goal-setting. An example of criteria for assessing discussion in an undergraduate class follows:

1. A minimum of three posts are made, at regular intervals (beginning, middle and end of discussion)
2. Contributions are succinct and professional, well-structured and easy to read
3. Posts are relevant to the topic and responsive to other participants
4. Links are made to personal experience and practice
5. Links are made to policy, theory and literature
6. Insights demonstrate depth and critique
7. Contributions are designed to move the discussion along, by sharing resources, posing questions for peers, or otherwise demonstrating leadership.

This is just one possible set of assessment criteria, developed through research and consultation with students and lecturers (Forbes, 2012, 2015). There are many ways to assess discussion, whether formatively or summatively, and these are discussed further in chapter 5 of this volume.

An additional way to conceptualise the purpose of AOD is to consider what it is not. That is, a contribution to online discussion is not an essay or a dissertation or thesis. The form of writing differs, in length, format and formality from these other types of academic writing. Neither is AOD a monologue or even a casual chat with friends. Ideally, AOD sits between verbal conversation and written discourse (Fear & Erikson-Brown, 2014). Part of purposeful AOD is the challenge of developing fluency in the language of the genre.

3.2 Develop Fluency in the Language of Discussion

The language of AOD tends to be a blend of speaking and writing, more spontaneous and flowing than formal writing, so as to be conversational. As a lean medium with fewer channels for transmission than face-to-face communication, the lack of visual and intonation cues in AOD is widely acknowledged, and was mentioned in Chapter 2. However, there are a variety of strategies participants can use to compensate for reduced social cues, including greetings and acknowledgments, emojis or emoticons, personal vignettes and self-disclosure. To communicate clearly in the online discussion, students are encouraged to remember the audience for their communications: their peers and teachers.

Locke and Daly (2007) explored the strategies used to establish and maintain relationships by participants in an online Masters level course using the framework of Politeness first developed by Brown and Levinson (1987). They analysed the frequency that five participants used of a range of verbal and nonverbal strategies in 219 exhanges across seven AODs which addressed the positive face, or the need to be liked or included. The politeness strategies included the use of the inclusive pronoun, 'we' or 'us' (e.g., "should *we* encourage divergent thinking…"), hedging statements made (e.g., "*For me, personally*, I don't find that totally ethically sufficient"), agreeing with other participants (e.g., *I totally agree with you all* that to foster students' interests to read…"), intensifciation of interest (e.g., "*I am really interested* in how you handle these problems in your teaching"), asserting common ground (e.g., " well we're on the same wavelength re NCEA…"), and sharing compliments (e.g., "*I think you summed the whole idea up well* when you said…").

Chen (2024), Liang's summer research student, conducted an analysis of the language used in AOD by undergraduate students, examining a sample of 98 discussion posts. Her investigation revealed a prevalent usage of linguistic devices such as greetings (e.g. *Hi xxx and Hello xxx*), expressions of appreciation (e.g. *useful, important* and *interesting*), and upscaled grading or intensifiers (e.g. *very, really* and *indeed*). Two-thirds of the posts commenced with a greeting, and even in self-initiated discussions, over 40% of posts incorporated a salutation. Expressions of appreciation were even more common, with a total of 88 instances observed across the sampled posts. Additionally, Liang observed a heavy reliance on the upscaled grading devices (intensifiers) to enhance the tone, with 70 instances of intensifiers identified, primarily employed in conveying appreciation and agreement.

In a similar vein, Forbes (2022) emphasised the need for discussion participants to acknowledge and respond to their peers. The students ($n = 7$) interviewed in Forbes' study reported a tendency to contribute more actively to discussion when peers responded to posts and questions. They suggested they would rather have their ideas actively challenged than ignored. Furthermore, students indicated they appreciated their names being used as part of peer-to-peer responsiveness. One student explained that writing a name in discussion is equivalent to looking at a peer in class, to pay attention and respond directly. Using people's names when responding is a direct social acknowledgement that communicates social presence by personalising the interaction and signalling active listening. The importance of personal acknowledgement as part of the relational character of communication has been reinforced by Lehman and Conceicao (2010), among others. Inclusion can be enhanced by acknowledging several peers in a single message, weaving and synthesising, and concluding a message with an invitation to the wider group to respond.

The language of discussion is necessarily succinct. Very long, rambling posts are likely to be overlooked, and cause irritation or confusion for peers. Keeping contributions brief allows space for others to add their ideas, enhancing the conversational exchange. Students admit that they rarely read posts that are too long or full of jargon, as these are perceived as unhelpful for learning. On the other hand, there is little point to a post without any meaningful content, and the online discussion is an excellent place to clarify and apply the specialist terminology of one's discipline. It is also a forum for sharing and making sense of ideas from literature and theory. In each case, however, this is best done by paraphrasing and aiming to be succinct. Lengthy quotes copied and pasted into the forum do not serve to demonstrate understanding nor to engage other participants. There is a balance to the in/formality of AOD, as it also differs from casual, social chatter, in terms of purpose, learning intent, and academic expectations. While expectations will vary, it is generally good form to check spelling and grammar in contributions, to ensure clarity. Breaking ideas up into paragraphs makes for ease of reading. There is a similar need to balance the time spent crafting a contribution, as this need not be painstaking, but neither is it wise to dash off a hasty response without some preparation and consideration of content, form, purpose, and audience.

3.3 Manage Time and Self

Students lead busy lives, juggling multiple responsibilities and pursuits. When life is busy, it is easy to forget the need to commit time and effort to online discussion, particularly when studying multiple classes, and managing competing deadlines. Planning time for discussion is essential, and likely to require time for noting and considering the topic, reading the contributions of others, reflecting, researching, and preparing one's own contributions. A good rule of thumb is to prepare for the discussion sooner rather than later, by being aware of the topic to allow time for thinking and research. Getting into the online discussion early is a wise approach, and a first post can often consist of initial thoughts about the topic, or relating prior knowledge before going away to read and research further. In the classes Dianne teaches, discussions can range for nine or ten days and students are required to make three well-spaced posts during this timeframe. This means posting a contribution near the start of the discussion, within the first two or three days, then returning mid-discussion to respond to others and build on ideas, and finally following up near the end of the discussion with concluding thoughts, and possibly a summary. These three posts can be planned to some extent in advance by formulating goals for each contribution. For example,

Beginning discussion—provide my thoughts on the topic, relate my own experience, invite others to share ideas.

Mid-discussion—read the contributions of others and respond, building upon their ideas. Respond to any questions or prompts from the lecturer or peers, add ideas from relevant literature and practice.

End of discussion—read and respond. Reflect upon the trajectory of the discussion and how ideas have changed, consider what new learning has occured. Suggest implications of this learning for ongoing practice.

Each of the three posts can be scheduled on a calendar, physical or electronic, and reminders can also be set to ensure the timelines are followed. This management of time and self is important to ensure active learning through discussion. As Jamie's story shows, if students forget about the discussion and make a late start, the forum can be overwhelming and opportunities to add value to the discussion may have passed. It can be challenging to think of new ideas to add. If multiple posts are required, making these on a single day can reduce the opportunity for reflecting between contributions. In cases where students add all three posts on the final day of discussion, the lapse in time and self management is readily apparent to others, and there is less opportunity for peers to respond or for ideas to be appreciated, challenged or built upon. This advice is supported by the work of Chen and Huang (2019), cited in Chapter 2, in relation to student prestige.

3.4 Add Value to the Discussion

If we accept that the purpose of AOD is to learn and to contribute to the learning of others, then it follows that adding value to discussion means working toward these goals. In order to learn through AOD, students are encouraged to contribute by asking questions, sharing thinking, trying out new ideas, and seeking to make links to prior knowledge. Following a similar pattern to the three-post guidance in the previous section, some examples of how students can add value to discussion are represented by the following prompts:

Before discussion—

- Familiarise yourself with the topic (question, scenario) represented by the discussion-starter.
- Brainstorm: What do you already know, do and understand in relation to the topic?
- Are there any specific examples or initial thoughts you might share in order to get the ball rolling?
- Are there questions or wonderings you can pose to help others to contribute their own shared or contrasting experiences?

Consider your next steps:

To move beyond these initial thoughts, what strategies will you engage in to advance your learning in relation to the topic? e.g., you might read the recommended literature; carry out some independent research; and continue to read contributions to the discussion for fresh ideas. You can continue the discussion offline in effect, by raising the topic with colleagues, family and friends in conversation, before returning to the online discussion to report on your wider conversations (within the boundaries of privacy of course). Very often, students will post in AOD by writing, "I asked my family about this last night at dinner, and their thoughts were…".

During the discussion—

- Read and consider the contributions of others as the discussion evolves.

- Consider which of the points you could respond to. It is helpful to acknowledge others, in order to build upon (rather than repeating) their points. It is often possible to notice patterns across the discussion—e.g., areas of similarity in thinking (agreement, converging ideas), and potentially issues, diverse perspectives and divergence. Pointing out patterns like this shows careful consideration and analysis of peers' contributions and can help to add new insights to the topic.
- Students can also respond directly to questions or prompts from other participants, as well as adding new questions and prompts. Alongside questioning, the sharing of relevant insights from ongoing research is often valued. Students will often share ideas from material they have recently read, heard or viewed. This can include course materials, but also frequently extends to independent research, and to incidental content discovered—for example, if you saw a news item of relevance to the topic, mentioning it in discussion can often be useful for others (particularly if you can hyperlink the item).
- Sharing diverse perspectives enriches discussion, and can be done by sharing personal experience, or the experience of other parties, real or imagined. For example, students can signal they are playing Devil's Advocate, or wondering if others might see a situation differently.

Ending the discussion—

As the discussion draws to a conclusion, it is valuable to take stock of the learning achieved during the discussion period. Returning to the forum to sum up and make a final contribution can assist with closure as well as goal-setting for future learning. Consider the following questions:

- What have I learned during this discussion?
- How has my thinking changed?
- What will I do next to continue to develop in this area?
- What questions remain for me?

3.5 Actively Seek Feedback

Novices to discussion very often seek reassurance that they are 'on the right track'. While these doubts are natural, and can be mitigated by clear purposes and expectations for discussion in the class, it is also possible for individuals to signal that they are seeking feedback on particular ideas. In practice, students often do this by including questions like the following in their contributions to AOD.

- Am I on the right track here?
- Does anyone have a different perspective?
- Has anyone found evidence to support or challenge these ideas?
- I welcome your thoughts.
- I look forward to reading others' ideas on this topic.

Phrases like the above serve to invite input from discussion partners, and convey an openness to new ideas. At the same time, if a discussion is genuinely rich and constructive, there are likely to be multiple tracks rather than a single way to approach it.

3.6 Take Safe Risks

It follows from the above that the learning potential of discussion lies with an individual's ability to reflect upon and re-evaluate knowledge claims. A student may start with initial thoughts on a topic, making links to prior experience, and this is a valuable starting point to usefully highlight at the start of a discussion. The point of learning is to move beyond this initial starting point, and often beyond one's own perspective, to an enlarged awareness of evidence, arguments, and multiple perspectives on any given topic. Fundamentally, to learn through discussion, we must be willing to share our thoughts, and then actively work to change views on the basis of new evidence and reasoning. Some of the evidence will come from our own investigations and research into the topic, which can be productively shared in the AOD. Other challenges will come through the discussion itself, as our discussion partners share their research and diverse perspectives. This is the essence of dialogic education, as introduced in chapter 1.

3.7 Challenge Politely

In any discussion, there will be divergent opinions and perspectives, and participants should be encouraged to ask questions and share doubts and disagreements (Locke & Daly, 2007). This interactive negotiation process allows participants to collaboratively explore the topic through rational analysis and problem-solving, which is recognised as the most effective talk type for knowledge construction (Mercer, 2000). The negotiation can be done respectfully, in keeping with netiquette and appreciative language. For example, it can be helpful to acknowledge and commend our discussion partners' ideas before presenting our own contrasting viewpoints. Again, helpful phrases can be a useful guide and contrastive conjunctions, like *but* and *however,* often serve as signposts here:

e.g.,

- My perspective on this issue may differ in some ways. I think…
- Another way of thinking about this could be…
- There is evidence for that side of the debate, however on the other hand,…

In summary, the following guidelines are based upon advice from experienced online learners to those who are new to AOD:

3.8 What You Are Expected to Do in Discussion

- Contribute to every discussion at regular intervals
- Keep each contribution to around 150 words max, as a guide
- Write in clear paragraphs, for ease of reading
- Check punctuation, grammar and spelling is accurate and appropriate to our classroom
- Respond to others in the discussion, building on ideas. Aim to ensure that others are acknowledged directly. Attempt to respond to different people throughout the discussion so as to be inclusive
- Connect with the topic and thread of the discussion. Either follow and extend the thread, or introduce a new direction. In either case, alter the title/subject of your contribution accordingly
- Share personal experience and perspectives of relevance to the discussion
- Use the discussion to clarify understanding, and to engage critically and deeply with the theme, theory and issues
- Be professional. Communicate respectfully. Demonstrate your understanding of cybersafety, netiquette and the underpinning rationale for our discussion. Respect alternative viewpoints, keep an open mind, and be prepared for challenge and change
- Aim to keep the discussion moving forward

In relation to readings, these should be completed regularly in order to construct familiarity with theory and diverse perspectives. When you refer to readings, avoid lengthy direct quotes in discussion. Instead, discuss readings by paraphrasing the key ideas and applying your own thinking to these. When directly using readings in discussion, it is not necessary to use full APA referencing if the reading is known to the class (e.g., it is from our readings list). In this case it is fine to use the author's name only. However, if using an original source, that others may be unacquainted with, a full reference should be provided to enable others to track down and follow up the reading if they want to. Where the resource/reading is available online, it is very helpful to include an active hyperlink in your post.

3.9 What You Should Avoid Doing—According to Feedback from Students

- Please do not avoid discussion, or post once and then disappear. These approaches breach the intent of discussion, indicate lack of regard for our class community and fall short of minimum attendance and participation requirements for effective learning online through AODs

- Similarly, do not double-post (2 consecutive posts, or posts very close together). While this may be necessary when 'life gets in the way', it is not ideal and if everyone did this, there would be no discussion occurring throughout the week, limiting the chances for reflection and response within our community. Please note that when responding to the ideas raised by others, it is best to do so in a single post mentioning others by name, rather than in a series of posts one after the other.
- Do not post lengthy contributions. Research suggests that your fellow students will not read posts if they are too long
- Do not post without firstly reading what others have said. This can be perceived as failing to listen to others and to acknowledge them as participants in the conversation
- Similarly, do not exclude others by responding to the same individuals every time you post
- Do not fixate on the personal. Although valued, it is a starting point. Your experiences are one set of possible experiences, and the goal is to begin with these as a starting point while looking more widely beyond the past or here and now
- Do not play it safe, agreeing with all and sundry. This does not assist in moving the discussion along. If you agree, say why and justify why your agreement matters
- Please do not take things personally. Don't be quick to take offence, but rather give others the benefit of the doubt. Remember that:

(a) others may be playing "devil's advocate" and proposing an extreme view in order to prompt thinking, and raise alternative perspectives;
(b) it is easy to misinterpret tone and intention online. Use emoticons purposefully in order to soften and convey a constructive mood.

3.10 What to Expect from Your Teachers in Our Online Discussions

Teachers aim to join in each discussion, meeting similar expectations to the students. In short, we aim to:

- Be there
- Be brief
- Respond
- Share our own stories
- Promote deep and critical thinking (at times, we will play 'Devil's Advocate' in order to probe differing viewpoints)
- Keep the fires burning

Feedback on discussion will be given within the discussion, formatively, so look out for teacher comments on how the discussion is progressing.

3.11 Scenario… Some Time Later

While watching a movie with friends, Jamie notices the main character in the film facing a challenge very similar to the problem being discussed in class this week. What a great illustration to share with my discussion group, thinks Jamie. I'll get online first thing in the morning and share this example, citing this movie. Setting a calendar alert, Jamie muses, Devon will find this example interesting following on from their post the other day, as it differs from the experience Devon told us about. I wonder what the others will think, and if they have seen this movie too…

References

Brown, P., & Levinson, S. (1987). *Politeness. some universals in language usage*. Cambridge University Press.

Chen, B., & Huang, T. (2019). It is about timing: Network prestige in asynchronous online discussions. *Journal of Computer Assisted Learning, 35*(4), 503–515.

Chen, M. (2024). *Interpersonal interaction in online discussion* [poster presentation]. Hamilton, New Zealand: University of Waikato.

Fear, W. J., & Erikson-Brown, A. (2014). Good quality discussion is necessary but not sufficient in asynchronous tuition: A brief narrative review of the literature. *Journal of Asynchronous Learning Networks JALN, 18*(2), 21. https://doi.org/10.24059/olj.v18i2.399

Forbes, D. (2012). Footprints participant perspectives informing pedagogy for asynchronous online discussion in initial teacher education. Thesis (Ph.D. Education)--University of Waikato, 2013.

Forbes, D. (2015). Legacies of learning: Negotiating guidelines for online discussion. In N. Wright, & D. Forbes (Eds.), Digital Smarts: Enhancing Learning and Teaching (pp. 82–103). Hamilton, New Zealand: Wilf Malcolm Institute of Educational Research.

Forbes, D., & Gedera, D. (2019). From confounded to common ground: misunderstandings between tertiary teachers and students in online discussions. *Australasian Journal of Educational Technology, 35*(4), p. 13. https://doi.org/10.14742/ajet.3595

Forbes, D. (2022). Student expectations of peers in academic asynchronous online discussion. *Journal of Open, Flexible and Distance Learning, 26*(1), 27–41. https://doi.org/10.61468/jofdl.v26i1.505

Lehman, R. M., & Conceicao, S. C. O. (2010). *Creating a sense of presence in online teaching*. Jossey-Bass.

Locke, T., & Daly, N. (2007). Towards congeniality: The place of politeness in asynchronous online discussion. *International Journal of Learning, 13*(12).

Mercer, N. (2000). *Words and Minds: How We Use Language to Think Together* (1st ed.). Routledge. https://doi.org/10.4324/9780203464984

Chapter 4
Effective Teaching Through Online Discussion—Enhancing Pedagogy and Practice

Abstract This chapter looks at how teachers can convene and moderate online discussions in ways that are effective for student learning and engagement; time-efficient; varied and satisfying. The chapter tackles basic organizational factors such as grouping, topics, links to class, and assignments, purpose/s, and how to guide students. A key point of reference is acknowledgement of common concerns for teachers as we strive to keep the online discussions interesting and varied, to engage student participation and promote learning. The chapter provides guidance on how to establish a purpose for discussion, maintain appropriate presence, intervene to enhance learning, and manage time and self effectively to keep workload under control.

A new undergraduate class was handed over to Shania, the lecturer, during the COVID pandemic. The class was designed with two lectures and one tutorial session each week. However, because of the pandemic, the majority of the students were off-campus, and the traditional face-to-face lectures and tutorials were no longer applicable. Shania had the option to deliver the lectures and tutorials on Zoom or record them using Panopto. But she had concerns that Zoom or recorded sessions might not be able to achieve the same results as F2F sessions as it is difficult to interact with students during talks and to supervise students during activities. She would like her students to be active rather than passive learners, to contribute rather than simply receiving the knowledge. Besides, it is also challenging for students to stay focused during the whole session, and even shorter recordings might not solve the problem. What alternative approach can be adopted to teach the class?

Asynchronous online discussion (AOD) can be used as a complement of or a replacement for lectures and tutorials. No matter what role discussions perform, the design should aim to maximise interaction and promote deep learning. To achieve this purpose, teachers need to create engaging and productive discussion starters, offer feedback throughout the discussion to prompt knowledge co-construction, and encourage reflection and summarisation towards the end of the discussion. In addition, teachers need to consider other issues related to discussion, such as the number of students in each group, the amount of teacher presence and the management of workload. In this chapter, we will first examine the teaching strategies implemented in the full cycle of discussion, that is, discussion starter, discussion intervention and discussion conclusion, and then look at other relevant issues.

4.1 Discussion Starter

The theme of a discussion is largely determined by its subject area and learning outcomes, but teachers still have the leeway to design their own discussion starters regarding both the topic of discussion and the type of discussion. Discussion starters tend to have a close relationship with the level of thinking (Oh et al., 2018), and according to Bloom's (1956) taxonomy, a well-crafted discussion topic should provoke higher-level thinking such as application, analysis, synthesis, and evaluation, rather than remaining at the level of memorisation or comprehension.

A potential pitfall in designing discussion starters is using activities with single or limited solutions (Nandi et al., 2012; Stavredes, 2011). Activities with single or limited solutions are commonly used in synchronous teaching sessions, but they are not the best choice for asynchronous discussions. Students may feel frustrated when they find little to add after a couple of early posts (Boettcher & Conrad, 2021). A typical case can be observed in the "more prescriptive, algorithmic, and more narrowly focused" programming course described by Nandi et al. (2012), in which the solution posted by one student often put an end to the discussion. Therefore, it is important for teachers to design both the topic and the type of activities to suit the context of asynchronous discussion.

4.1.1 Discussion Topic

The discussion topic is the subject or theme for group interaction. In order to enhance the productivity of discussions, teachers are advised to select topics that are open-ended and exploratory (Boettcher & Conrad, 2021). These topics can be drawn from real-life experiences or external resources, providing students with the opportunity to explore different viewpoints and reflect on their own positions. By encouraging diverse perspectives and critical thinking, these discussion topics can foster greater engagement and develop a deeper understanding of the subject.

Activities related to real-life situations have been suggested by many researchers as a productive starter (e.g. Bender, 2012; Brookfield & Preskill, 2005; Fear & Erikson-Brown, 2014; Kilis & Yildirim, 2019; Nandi et al., 2012). Bender (2012) suggests that knowledge is constructed from real-life experience and prior learning. Brookfield & Preskill (2005) believe that the relationship between discussion topics and real life determines the motivation of participation. Kilis and Yildirim (2019)

4.1 Discussion Starter

found that topics addressing real-life experiences and encouraging self-disclosure of students promoted open communication, enhanced group cohesion, and stimulated deep learning. Nandi et al. (2012) argue that the examples of personal and work life provided by the students broaden the scope of the discussion. They also found that more questions and answers were generated by real world situations in their introductory IT course in comparison with a fact-based programming one.

Real-life situations can be included in many different activities. One simple but important one is to ask students to introduce themselves, which has been used widely at the beginning of almost all online courses as discussed in chapter 2. The activity realises the second stage of Gilly Salmon's (2011) five-stage online learning model, online socialisation, and aligns with the third Māori value, Whanaungatanga or relationships, as outlined in Rātima et al.'s (2022) cultural responsiveness model in chapter 2. Through self-introduction, students establish their own identities, familiarise themselves with the online learning environment, connect with fellow learners, and foster mutual trust and respect, getting ready for their online learning. Another activity is to ask students to talk about their attitudes, beliefs, and knowledge about the subject-related discussion topic, or to relate the course content to what they know. The activity not only helps teachers identify the current knowledge level of their students, but also allows students the space to establish personalised connections and make individualised contributions. Discussion can be built upon these personal stories by examining them from a different perspective or understanding them at a new level (Brookfield & Preskill, 2005).

Activities that take advantage of external resources, such as websites, videos and apps, can also serve as effective discussion starters. Fear and Erikson-Brown (2014) proposed the use of external resources as another design that promoted interaction, alongside real-life-based design. An example is to motivate students to search and share online resources related to the chosen topic. This approach empowers every learner to construct their knowledge in a personalised way with the support of a vast number of resources available online. Students are then asked to comment on key issues raised by the shared resources. Another example of this type can be the one that invites students to teach something to their groups with the use of online articles, images, videos or even with their self-created resources. In order to foster higher-order thinking, students are encouraged to raise questions about others' teaching content.

4.1.2 Discussion Type

In addition to discussion topics, the type of discussion is another critical factor for a productive discussion. Open-ended activities (Oh et al., 2018; Richardson & Ice, 2010; York & Richardson, 2012), controversial activities (Howell et al., 2017; Richardson & Ice, 2010; York & Richardson, 2012), and case study/problem-solving activities (Fear & Erikson-Brown, 2014; Kilis & Yildirim, 2019; Oh et al., 2018;

Richardson & Ice, 2010) are often proposed as the most common and most effective types of discussion starters. Open-ended discussions invite students to explore a particular concept, a topic, a belief, an experience, or an issue. For example, when teaching translation, teachers can ask students to discuss "what is your idea of a good translation" and to explain their ideas with examples. When introducing the apps for learning, teachers can ask students to share the features of their favourite app that promotes learning.

Controversial discussion activities or debates encourage students to explain and defend their position, and to think critically and argue against the other position(s). A good example is McDonald et al.'s (2012) provocative prompts, in which quotations from various perspectives are used to challenge students' opinions and prepare them for disagreement. Students are asked to explain the reasons why one quotation resonates with them, and another one irritates them. At the end of the activity, they share new insights gained from reading all the posts. Howell et al.'s (2017) Focal Prompt is another good example of controversial tasks. In this study, students were presented with five different constructivist instructional design models. They are challenged to choose the most useful one for a given work situation and to provide a rationale for their choice. The Focal Prompt proves to be the most effective one in facilitating learning in comparison to the other two prompts in the study, namely describing the application of a model or brainstorming different applications of a model. Likewise, controversial task design can be used in teaching multiple linear regression in statistics. Teachers can ask students to choose the best regression model among many possibilities and to justify their choice on the basis of their statistical knowledge and real-life experiences.

As a form of controversial task, debate typically requires students to critically evaluate two opposing positions on a given issue. The topic of the debate in Richardson and Ice's (2010) study is "whether today's learners should be taught differently because they have access to various technologies". Although their debate task was not as well received as the open-ended discussion among students, it promoted higher levels of thinking, with 78% of the students who participated in the debate reaching the integration and resolution levels, compared to 61% of those who engaged in the open-ended discussion. In addition to fostering critical thinking, the experienced online teacher featured in York and Richardson's (2012) study contends that controversial topics can also enhance student engagement and interaction. In our digital learning course, Dianne allocated students into a negative and an affirmative team to engage in a debate about the educational value and potential drawbacks of digital games and gaming. More examples would be *Cellphone bans in schools, as mandated by governments around the world. Are there more democratic alternatives?* And *Artificial intelligence—academic integrity and creative affordances.* This kind of controversial topic can also arise from media coverage, allowing students to identify current events that relate to the course/discussion topic, and share relevant news articles to spark discussion and debate. The beauty of these discussions is that they are driven by students' interests and choices and evolve over time as new topics emerge in the news.

A case study approach, "bridging the gap between theory and practice" (Barkley et al., 2014, p. 238), can help students better understand and cope with real-life situations. Cases or scenarios are often used as a problem-based learning approach. In the study by Kilis and Yildirim (2019), six cases (i.e. students' initial student experiences using computers, overuse of social networking services, computer-based learning experiences, digital information safety, online search strategies, and sense of community) were chosen to teach computer literacy. All the cases addressed the day-to-day situations of those students, who were encouraged to share the challenges or problems they faced, the strategies or skills they resorted to, and the suggestions or solutions they could give to their fellow students. The inclusion of these cases resulted in a high level of social and cognitive presence. Richard and Ice (2010) found that although the case study was not the most preferred learning approach of their students, it stimulated the highest level of thinking compared to open-ended discussion and debate. An example of the use of scenario can be found in Oh et al. (2018) where students were presented with a dilemma regarding whether or not to include customers' views while evaluating a customer service training programme in an organisation. Then they were asked to choose one side of the dilemma and justify their selection. Like case studies, this scenario-based discussion task was found to promote cognitive presence at a higher level, and thus to contribute to deep learning as discussed in Chapter 1.

4.2 Discussion Intervention

During a discussion, teachers play a critical role in facilitating and guiding the conversation, by overseeing its progression, nurturing student participation, and motivating students to continue engaging with the topic. According to the literature, teachers can consider six types of intervention to stimulate discussions. These are maintaining momentum with the use of questions (Brookfield & Preskill, 2005; Forbes, 2012; Kwon et al., 2019), acknowledging students' contributions (Brookfield & Preskill, 2005; Forbes, 2012), correcting students' posts (Brookfield & Preskill, 2005; Forbes, 2012; Hoey, 2017), sharing new information including resources, experiences, and opinions (Forbes, 2012; Hoey, 2017), summarising key points during the discussion (Clark & Bartholomew, 2014; Forbes, 2012), and modelling and providing guidance for discussion (Forbes, 2012; Stavredes, 2011).

4.2.1 Maintaining Momentum with the use of Questions

Questions can be used to request more evidence, ask for clarification, elicit different perspectives, link back to previous posts, and review what has been covered (Brookfield & Preskill, 2005). Examples are:

- What additional evidence can you find to support…?,
- Tell us more about…?,
- What else do we need to consider in regard to…?,
- How does your contribution add to …?, and
- What has surprised you in this week's discussion?.

According to Forbes (2012), students value and benefit from the questions asked halfway through a discussion as they serve as catalysts to keep the discussion moving forward. Similarly, Kwon et al. (2019) propose that the number of elaboration-type of questions asked in a discussion is positively correlated to interactivity, while the number of perspective-widening-type of questions correlates with a high level of knowledge construction.

4.2.2 Acknowledging Students' Contributions

Acknowledgements, especially personal acknowledgement with individual names, are appreciated by students as it indicates the teacher has noticed and is interested in their particular post and intends to foster a connection with that student (Forbes, 2012). Brookfield & Preskill, (2005) advise teachers to distinguish appreciation from praise to thank students for their participation and to specifically praise them for their distinct and concrete contributions. One of the dangers of acknowledging students is excessive affirmation. Clark and Bartholomew (2014) found teachers' acknowledgements took up one-third of the teacher comments and at the same time teachers did not provide sufficient challenges for the students. Besides acknowledgements, teachers can offer corrections or challenge students with alternative perspectives as discussed below.

4.2.3 Correcting Students' Posts

Alongside positive feedback students also expect teachers to disagree with them and correct their mistakes (Forbes, 2012). Teacher feedback can act as constructive challenge to complement students' posts or even to contrast with their opinions (Brookfield & Preskill, 2005). In order to remain positive and supportive, teachers can position the feedback in terms of "devil's advocacy" or to say "here is another perspective". It is important to prepare students for the possibility of challenge via the discussion guidelines, as noted in chapter 3. It is also beneficial to encourage students to challenge each other's points and to teach them how to do this in a polite and respectful way. The debate/role play gamification of discussion can enable this. Sometimes it might be more appropriate to send the feedback directly to the student rather than post it publicly in the discussion forum (Hoey, 2017). Teachers can send private messages to the particular student to point out his or her mistakes and provide a general comment in the discussion forum to correct misunderstandings, to avoid embarrassment for that student.

4.2.4 Sharing New Information Including Resources, Experiences, and Opinions

Teachers, as subject experts, are expected to provide information and informed perspectives (Hew, 2015; Westberry & Franken, 2013). At the same time, students may expect teachers to share their personal experiences and viewpoints to model reciprocity (Forbes, 2012). The self-disclosure of teachers was reported to significantly improve students' perceptions of the teacher and the course, and to slightly increase student achievement (Hoey, 2017), which also links to relationships and openness.

4.2.5 Summarising Key Points During the Discussion

A paragraph of summary, though cannot replace teacher input at various points throughout the discussion, is regarded as a helpful means to recapitulate crucial ideas and to provide a foundation for future discussion (Forbes, 2012). It is important for teachers to pay more attention to the summary category, as it tends to be overlooked. Clark and Bartholomew (2014) found that none of five teachers in their study gave any consideration to the summary aspect. Teachers can either summarise the discussion themselves or prompt students to commence the summary, and then fill in any gaps with feedback. In the case of role play discussed in chapter 6, one student can be allocated the "summariser" role, tasked with periodically summarising on the way through the discussion, as well as in conclusion.

4.2.6 Modelling and Providing Guidance for Discussion

The teacher's participation itself sets a model of good practice. In addition to modelling, students also expect clear guidance from teachers (Forbes, 2012). Model posts and specific guidance can help prompt discussion, particularly at the beginning of discussion when students may feel apprehensive (Stavredes, 2011). Feedback on discussion process/progress can be provided alongside instructional support. As shown in chapter 2, discussion guidelines can clearly stipulate what students can expect from their teachers. In this way, there is a reciprocity between communicating clear expectations to students and undertaking to be present and active as a teacher in the online discussion.

Although there are six types of discussion intervention, in many cases a single post often includes more than one type of intervention, as demonstrated in the short post below, which Liang wrote in response to one of the students in her translation class:

> Hello XX, drawing is an excellent example, and I appreciate you bringing it up. [acknowledgement] As we know, different people will have diverse interpretations of the same artwork, which shows that there are a thousand Hamlets in the eyes of a thousand people. [sharing information] It is fascinating to consider that we all have our own versions of translation, and I personally view translation as a creative process. [sharing opinion]
>
> However, we must also keep in mind that as translators, we cannot deviate too far from the source text. [sharing opinion] So what principle do you suggest we follow? [elaboration] Can you provide us with an example to clarify your perspective? [elaboration] I encourage others to share their opinions on this matter as well. [guidance]

4.3 Discussion Conclusion

When a discussion comes to an end, it is time to wrap it up. A discussion conclusion can take two forms: teacher-led or student-led (Boettcher & Conrad, 2021). Teachers can close discussion threads by posting a wrap-up post, creating an audio or video summary, or including the conclusion in a synchronous session. Teachers can also involve students in this higher-level thinking task. Individual students can take turns to conclude and reflect on different modules throughout the course or they can work in groups and each group collaboratively develops a conclusion. A conclusion can take different forms or combine different forms such as a list of essential points, a thought-provoking question, a visual representation of the subject matter or a memorable quote. It is important to establish an online platform like Moodle Glossary or allocate time in class for students to share their conclusions and receive feedback from teachers and peers. This approach allows teachers to address key messages of the discussion, correct any misconceptions, gather unanswered questions for future consideration, create a bridge to the next learning activity and prompt students to look ahead.

4.4 Variables Contributing to the Success of Online Discussion

Besides design, guidance, and wrap-up, the success of online discussions can be influenced by many other factors. In the following sections we will discuss group size, the frequency of teacher intervention and the workload of teachers, as these important factors have been extensively discussed in the literature.

4.4.1 Group Size

The size of the group is a key factor in discussion design that can potentially affect student engagement and learning performance. The size of a discussion group is primarily influenced by the purpose of the discussion and the profile of students. Whole-class discussion with 30 or more students exposes students to rich information and divergent perspectives, leading to a broad understanding of the topic and potentially challenging their beliefs (Chen & Liu, 2020; Qiu & McDougall, 2015). This approach is frequently utilised in MOOCs, where a large number of learners can benefit from a wide variety of posts to read and the freedom to directly participate or observe as an 'active lurker' without contributing to the discussion. As Yang et al. (2022) suggested, active lurkers, in particular, appreciate the benefits of a whole-class discussion such as "comprehensive analysis, innovative solutions, multiple perspectives, and opportunities for idea synthesis and critical evaluation" (p.123). Despite these advantages, whole-class discussion tends to overwhelm students with an excessive amount of information, frustrate them with repetitive ideas, deter them from in-depth participation, and impede their ability to establish social connections with each other (Qiu & McDougall, 2015). If these disadvantages outweigh the advantages, small group discussion may be a better option. The optimal size of group can vary between 20–30 (Kim, 2013), 8–12 (Hew & Cheung, 2012; Tomei, 2006; Yang et al., 2022) or 3–5 participants (Boettcher & Conrad, 2021; Brookfield & Preskill, 2005; Hambacher et al, 2018; Qiu & McDougall, 2015). Small group configuration reduces information workload, encourages participation, and strengthens group cohesion (Kim, 2013; Qiu & McDougall, 2015). Within a small group, individual participants tend to stay focused and repeat less (Qiu & McDougall, 2015), feel more obliged to contribute (Yang et al., 2022), and connect and collaborate more with their peers (Kim, 2013; Qiu & McDougall, 2015). Yang et al. (2022) found that students in small groups read more discussion posts and wrote longer posts. If the option of viewing other groups' posts is provided, students can hear the perspectives of other groups when they choose to (Qiu & McDougall, 2015). However, the smaller the group size, the more likely the discussion is dominated by one or two group members and the more likely the teacher faces the dilemma of presence (Qiu & McDougall, 2015). With only a handful of students in the group, the teacher posting runs the risk of dominating the group discussion excessively and a dominant teacher can end the discussion prematurely by adding their thoughts as the last authoritative voice, as discussed in chapter 2.

When forming groups, it is also important to consider student profiles, as student participation largely depends on the participation of their peers (Chen & Liu, 2020; Forbes, 2022). Factors such as age, level of engagement, and previous online learning experiences can influence the effectiveness of online discussion. If the students are mature, active and experienced online learners, a smaller group could be a viable option. Otherwise, a larger group might be more appropriate to ensure sufficient input and interaction in the forum. Ultimately, each class is distinct, and the group size should be tailored to best suit the needs of the learners.

4.4.2 Frequency of Teacher Posts

Teacher presence has been a focus of previous studies, and among them many (e.g. Murphy & Fortner, 2014; Oh et al., 2018; Phirangee et al., 2016) have examined the effects of teacher-facilitated discussion versus peer-facilitated discussion, which has also been discussed in chapter 2. Oh et al. (2018) found peer-facilitated discussion more effective in fostering critical thinking and promoting interaction. Teacher posts were more likely to restrict students from presenting their different perspectives and to intimidate students from participation. Murphy and Fortner (2014) also found that teacher intervention did not improve the quality of postings but resulted in a lower number of student posts. They attributed it to the students' reliance on their teacher. However, both studies were in the context of blended learning and online discussions were not the only major venue for communicating with teachers. The research setting of Oh et al. (2018) is a graduate-level online course, which consists of both synchronous sessions (two hours each week) and asynchronous discussions. The course investigated by Murphy and Fortner (2014) comprised lectures and online discussion sessions. Inclusion of regular synchronous sessions might compensate for student needs for teacher presence during online discussions. Unlike the above two studies, Phirangee et al. (2016) chose eight online courses delivered mainly through online discussion. In comparison to peer-facilitated courses, teacher-facilitated courses led to more active participation with more posts and replies, and more editing, linking and rereading actions. The students had a stronger sense of community, cared more about their peers and were more interested in connecting with their peers. Students in the peer-facilitated courses tended to share their posts privately and message directly to their teachers. Although they also understood the importance of interaction, the motivation for their participation was to meet the course requirements. Phirangee et al. (2016) believe teachers' constant surveillance might contribute to the level of student participation.

Beyond the influencing factors of group size and teacher posts, many studies have investigated the reasons for the need for teacher presence. Six primary reasons have been provided across these studies, with the first three reasons being associated with the teacher's role as a subject expert, and the last three reasons pertaining to the role of a discussion moderator.

1. Share information and perspectives (Forbes, 2012; Hew, 2015)
2. Provide regular feedback (Forbes, 2012; Hew, 2015; Nandi et al., 2012; Phirangee et al., 2016)
3. Extend or direct discussion (Forbes, 2012; Hew, 2015; Nandi et al., 2012)
4. Model discussion strategies (Forbes, 2012)
5. Keep the discussion on track and ensure equity in the discussion (Forbes, 2012; Hew, 2015; Nandi et al., 2012; Phirangee et al., 2016)
6. Motivate students' participation (Forbes, 2012; Hew, 2015; Phirangee et al., 2016)

The presence of the teacher is crucial in asynchronous online discussion. When teachers are noticeably absent, students may start to question their teachers' level of engagement, longing for feedback and reassurance, struggling to see the relevance of discussion, and feeling lack of reciprocity interaction, which could eventually lead to the doubt on the value of their own efforts (Forbes, 2012). However, at the same time, teacher presence must be balanced with student presence (Fear & Erikson-Brown, 2014). Teachers, if sharing too much of his or her perspective at an early stage, may hinder students from posting their diverse ideas (Stavredes, 2011). It is necessary for teachers to periodically stand back to allow students time to reflect and space to express their ideas (Forbes, 2012). There is no clear guideline for ideal teacher participation. One of the suggestions from Forbes's (2012) interviews is that students expect their teachers to maintain a similar level of participation to the expected level of them. Open communication with students is needed to find out their expectations and to negotiate the reciprocal activity (Forbes, 2012).

4.4.3 Teacher Workload

Given the diverse expectations placed upon online teachers and the flexibility of online discussions, it is crucial to consider teacher workload. Although there is no agreement in the literature on the workload of e-learning teachers (Bright, 2015), teaching online can be a demanding task, especially when fewer teaching staff are expected to cater for a larger number of students in many tertiary institutions (Earl, 2015). This section will outline a number of strategies to address this challenge, focusing on three key areas: online presence, student leadership and feedback management.

Online teaching requires regular attention and a key strategy for teachers is to attend discussions "little but often" (Bright, 2015). Teachers can develop a routine by allocating regular time slots throughout working days (Stavredes, 2011). It is important not to interact with students outside their working hours to prevent the expectation of being "24/7 lecturers" (Bright, 2015). As the course progresses, teachers may gradually reduce input to encourage independent learning and student leadership (Bright, 2015).

Student leadership is crucial to the success of online teaching. With clear guidance, students can take different roles such as moderating discussions (Bright, 2015; Stavredes, 2011), providing feedback, answering each other's questions (Bright, 2015), and even participating in the course design process (Forbes, 2015). More details will be covered in chapter 6.

Feedback can take different forms. A discussion rubric can not only provide students with clear expectations but also allow teachers to start their feedback from a template (Boettcher & Conrad, 2021). Feedback in the form of audio or video reduces writing time (Bright, 2015). Additionally, group feedback can save teachers from responding to individual students by addressing the common misunderstandings and highlighting the desired participation (Boettcher & Conrad, 2021).

In this chapter we have explored the teaching strategies implemented in the full cycle of discussion, including the topics and types of discussion starters, discussion interventions, discussion conclusions and the variables contributing to the success of online discussions. In our next chapter we will discuss the applications of online discussion in both formative and summative contexts. The tensions arising from the interplay between formative and summative assessment will also be examined.

4.5 Return to Vignette

Finally, let's revisit the vignette where Shania faces the challenge of selecting a suitable teaching approach for her off-campus students. Shania decided to experiment with asynchronous online discussions after discussing with fellow lecturers, consulting with e-learning designers, and studying discussion design guides. She redesigned the course platform, created forums for self-introduction and online interaction, and worked out a range of discussion topics and online netiquette to start with. During discussion, she enjoyed the engaging conversations with students and often found herself inspired by the insightful ideas exchanged among her students.

4.6 Takeaway Tips

Incorporating online discussions into teaching can be both challenging and rewarding for teachers. It provides students with a space to engage and participate actively in their learning process. To effectively utilise online discussions, teachers need to consider the following tips:

- Elicit real-life experiences or external resources: Encourage students to draw from their own experiences or bring in external resources to enrich the discussions. This helps create a dynamic and diverse exchange of ideas.
- Design open-ended, controversial, or problem-solving activities: Craft discussion prompts that stimulate critical thinking and promote thoughtful dialogue. Open-ended questions, controversial topics, or problem-solving activities can encourage students to explore different perspectives and develop their analytical skills.
- Strategically guide and facilitate discussions: Teachers play a crucial role in shaping the flow of discussions. Provide milestone questions, offer feedback, and intervene when necessary to steer the conversation in productive directions.
- Highlight key points of discussions: Summarise and highlight the key takeaways from the discussions to ensure that important ideas are reinforced and understood by all participants. This can be done through providing written summaries or verbal recaps.
- Consider other factors: Factors such as class size, frequency of teacher intervention, and teacher workload should be taken into account. Adjusting the level of teacher involvement, creating discussion groups of appropriate size, or setting specific timeframes for discussions can help manage these factors effectively.

By following these steps, teachers can harness the power of online discussions to create an interactive and engaging learning environment that fosters critical thinking, collaboration, and knowledge sharing among students.

References

Barkley, E. F., Major, C. H., & Cross, K. P. (2014). Collaborative learning techniques: A handbook for college faculty (2nd ed.). Wiley & Sons, Inc.

Bender, T. (2012). *Discussion-Based Online Teaching to Enhance Student Learning : Theory, Practice and Assessment*. Stylus Publishing, LLC. http://ebookcentral.proquest.com/lib/waikato/detail.action?docID=987038

Bloom, B. S. (1956). *Taxonomy of educational objectives: Cognitive and affective domains*. David McKay.

Boettcher, J. V., & Conrad, R-M. (2021). *The Online Teaching Survival Guide: Simple and Practical Pedagogical Tips*. Wiley.

Bright, S. (2015). ELearning lecturer workload: Working harder or working smarter? In N. Wright & D. Forbes (Eds.), *Digital smarts: Enhancing learning and teaching* (pp. 161–178). Wilf Malcolm Institute of Educational Research.

Brookfield, S. D., & Preskill, S. (2005). *Discussion as a way of teaching: Tools and techniques for democratic classrooms*. Jossey-Bass.

Chen, L.-T., & Liu, L. (2020). Social presence in multidimensional online discussion: the roles of group size and requirements for discussions. *Computers in the Schools, 37*(2), 116–140. https://doi.org/10.1080/07380569.2020.1756648

Clarke, L. W., & Bartholomew, A. (2014). Digging beneath the surface: Analyzing the complexity of instructors' participation in asynchronous discussion [Report]. *Online Learning Journal (OLJ), 18*, 105+. https://link-gale-com.ezproxy.waikato.ac.nz/apps/doc/A443459164/AONE?u=waikato&sid=bookmark-AONE&xid=b4c0bd09

Earl, K. (2015). Assessment digital smarts: Using short text assignment formats for enhancing student learning. In N. Wright & D. Forbes (Eds.), *Digital smarts: Enhancing learning and teaching* (pp. 66–81). Wilf Malcolm Institute of Educational Research.

Fear, W. J., & Erikson-Brown, A. (2014). Good quality discussion is necessary but not sufficient in asynchronous tuition: A brief narrative review of the literature. *Journal of asynchronous learning networks JALN, 18*(2), 21. https://doi.org/10.24059/olj.v18i2.399

Forbes, D. (2012). *Footprints participant perspectives informing pedagogy for asynchronous online discussion in initial teacher education*. Thesis (Ph.D. Education)--University of Waikato, 2013.

Hambacher, E., Ginn, K., & Slater, K. (2018). Letting students lead: Preservice teachers' experiences of learning in online discussions. *Journal of Digital Learning in Teacher Education, 34*(3), 151–165. https://doi.org/10.1080/21532974.2018.1453893

Hew, K. F., & Cheung, W. S. (2012). *Student Participation in Online Discussions: Challenges, Solutions, and Future Research* (1. Aufl. ed.). Springer-Verlag. https://doi.org/10.1007/978-1-4614-2370-6

Hew, K. F. (2015). Student perceptions of peer versus instructor facilitation of asynchronous online discussions: Further findings from three cases. *Instructional Science, 43*(1), 19–38. https://doi.org/10.1007/s11251-014-9329-2

Hoey, R. (2017). Examining the characteristics and content of instructor discussion interaction upon student outcomes in an online course. *Online learning (Newburyport, Mass.), 21*(4), 263–281. https://doi.org/10.24059/olj.v21i4.1075

Howell, G. S., LaCour, M. M., & McGlawn, P. A. (2017). Constructing student knowledge in the online classroom: The effectiveness of focal prompts. *College Student Journal, 51*(4), 483–490.

Kilis, S., & Yildirim, Z. (2019). Posting patterns of students' social presence, cognitive presence, and teaching presence in online learning. *Journal of Asynchronous Learning Networks JALN, 23*(2), 179.

Kim, J. (2013). Influence of group size on students' participation in online discussion forums. *Computers and Education, 62*, 123–129. https://doi.org/10.1016/j.compedu.2012.10.025

Kwon, K., Park, S. J., Shin, S., & Chang, C. Y. (2019). Effects of different types of instructor comments in online discussions. *Distance Education, 40*(2), 226–242. https://doi.org/10.1080/01587919.2019.1602469

McDonald, J. P. (2012). *Going online with protocols: New tools for teaching and learning.* Teachers College Press.

Murphy, C. A., & Fortner, R. A. (2014). Impact of instructor intervention on the quality and frequency of student discussion posts in a blended classroom. *Journal of Online Learning and Teaching, 10*(3), 337.

Nandi, D., Hamilton, M., & Harland, J. (2012). Evaluating the quality of interaction in asynchronous discussion forums in fully online courses. *Distance Education, 33*(1), 5–30. https://doi.org/10.1080/01587919.2012.667957

Oh, E. G., Huang, W-H. D., Hedayati Mehdiabadi, A., & Ju, B. (2018). Facilitating critical thinking in asynchronous online discussion: comparison between peer-and instructor-redirection. *Journal of computing in higher education, 30*(3), 489-509. https://doi.org/10.1007/s12528-018-9180-6

Phirangee, K., Epp, C. D., & Hewitt, J. (2016). Exploring the relationships between facilitation methods, students' sense of community, and their online behaviors. *Online Learning, 20*(2), 134–154.

Qiu, M., & McDougall, D. (2015). Influence of group configuration on online discourse reading. *Computers and Education, 87*, 151–165. https://doi.org/10.1016/j.compedu.2015.04.006

Richardson, J. C., & Ice, P. (2010). Investigating students' level of critical thinking across instructional strategies in online discussions. *The Internet and Higher Education, 13*(1), 52–59. https://doi.org/10.1016/j.iheduc.2009.10.009

Salmon, G. (2011). *E-moderating: the key to teaching and learning online* (Third edition. ed.). Routledge. https://doi.org/10.4324/9780203816684

Stavredes, T. (2011). *Effective online teaching foundations and strategies for student success.* Wiley.

Tomei, L. A. (2006). The impact of online teaching on faculty load: Computing the ideal class size for online courses. *Journal of Technology and Teacher Education, 14*(3), 531.

Westberry, N., & Franken, M. (2013). Co-construction of knowledge in tertiary online settings: An ecology of resources perspective. *Instructional Science, 41*(1), 147–164. https://doi.org/10.1007/s11251-012-9222-9

Yang, T., Luo, H., & Sun, D. (2022). Investigating the combined effects of group size and group composition in online discussion. *Active Learning in Higher Education, 23*(2), 115–128. https://doi.org/10.1177/1469787420938524

York, C. S., & Richardson, J. C. (2012). Interpersonal interaction in online learning: Experienced online instructors' perceptions of influencing factors. *Journal of asynchronous learning networks JALN, 16*(4), 83–98. https://doi.org/10.24059/olj.v16i4.229

Chapter 5
Assessment Issues and Practices

Abstract This chapter outlines the formative and summative uses of online discussion, with examples of each. Assessment is often a contentious issue, not least because summative assessment can constrain students' participation and their enjoyment of discussion, inhibiting their expression of genuine views. Tensions between formative and summative assessment are explored, with a view to promoting deep learning. The practice of grading participation is critiqued, balanced with the need to motivate students. Formatively, discussion can function as interactive formative assessment, where students and teachers give and receive feedback and feedforward, in a timely fashion. Importantly, teachers are not the only source of such feedback, and peer and self-assessment can happen alongside teachers' monitoring discussions to identify and address misconceptions and to extend ideas.

We have been teaching online in a tertiary setting for over 50 years collectively, and in this time, we've developed our own individual approaches to assessment online. When reflecting on the assignments she sets, Nicola says three distinctive features are that she (1) tries to recognise online participation in a significant piece of assessment; (2) she aims for a variety of ways for her students to show what they know; and (3) she aims to scaffold the assignments. Nicola finds that when her students are asked each week to respond to key ideas in the lecture and readings for the week, they are simultaneously building their academic voice, and ideas which can be incorporated in either written essays, or Pechakucha presentations. As they express their own ideas and read those of their classmates, she believes they are slowly building up the ability to express their ideas about concepts from lectures and ideas in readings which are all chosen to support the topics being covered and being used in assignments. Dianne reflects that in a digital learning context, online discussion is a key skill to focus on, so it needs to be valued appropriately. This entails a significant weighting in summative assessment, with clear criteria communicated to students. As noted in chapter 3, Dianne uses seven basic criteria to guide and assess discussion, derived from research (Forbes, 2012, 2015). These cover regularity of contributions, clarity of posts, responsiveness to others, sharing of relevant personal/ professional experience, connections to literature, critical reflection, and leadership of discussion (e.g. by posing questions to encourage peer contributions). Like Nicola, Dianne ensures the online discussions build understanding that will help for other assignments and uses discussion as a means of interactive formative assessment by affirming and challenging students' thinking in the course of the discussions. Similar to Nicola and Dianne, Liang marks online discussions as a standalone assessment and at the same time she incorporates discussions into her other assignments. Online discussions serve as a platform for students to expand and enrich their understanding of other assigned tasks. Online discussions facilitate effective communication and collaboration among students, particularly in group work scenarios. Additionally, the posts generated during online discussions serve as valuable language data for the language analysis assignment in the course. The alignment of discussion topics with other assignments, and the use of online discussions as a means of collaboration and as a primary source of data create a holistic and cohesive learning experience, fostering an environment where students are not only motivated to participate in discussions but also appreciate and value the insights and contributions of their peers.

This chapter will outline the formative and summative uses of online discussion, with examples of each from tertiary students and tertiary teachers. Tensions between formative and summative assessment will be explored. Since assessment influences both how students spend their time and the type of learning taking place, the challenge is to assess in such a way as to encourage deep as opposed to surface approaches to learning. Solutions across a range of options and contexts are proposed in this chapter.

5.1 Learning and Assessment

Learning and assessment are key issues in the AOD-related literature. We discuss these issues together due to the element of learning contained in assessment, and due to the primacy of assessment for formative (learning) purposes as an aspect of pedagogy. We suggest that learning is at the heart of participant AOD experiences. For this reason, it is important to acknowledge the emphasis in the literature on deep learning, as opposed to surface learning, an emphasis that has permeated our guidance for students and teachers in chapters 3 and 4. Deep learning is characterised by striving to understand, to make sense, and to learn actively, leading to conceptual development and change as a person (Ellis et al, 2008). As such, deep learning requires higher order cognitive processing, including critical thinking and self-direction (Garrison & Anderson, 2003). Deep learning entails learners coming to see things differently (Haythornthwaite & Andrews, 2011; Holmes & Gardner, 2006; Loughran, 2006) and is often an outcome of dialogic learning as discussed in chapter 1.

It may be a challenge to measure or assess the extent to which students come to view teaching and learning differently, which could be why AOD assessment sometimes focuses more on surface features like quantifying participation rather than on the demonstration of deep learning. Assessment is often a contentious issue, not least because assessment can constrain students' participation and their enjoyment of discussion, inhibiting their expression of genuine views (Askell-Williams & Lawson, 2005; Fauske & Wade, 2003; Forbes, 2012; Locke, 2007).

5.2 Grading for Attendance and Participation

As already mentioned, a common approach to AOD assessment is to grade for attendance and participation. Arend (2007) notes the typicality of this approach and the reasoning behind it:

> Online, the instructor cannot tell whether the student is in attendance unless he or she is actively contributing something to the virtual class. As a result, online instructors grade for participation, typically between 10 and 25% of the course grade for discussion participation. (p. 3)

Discussion is often graded on a weekly basis, although Liang found that this imposed a very heavy workload on the teacher especially with large classes. Weekly grading is designed to make students participate all the way through their course, much like taking a roll in a face-to-face class (Arend, 2007). Other teachers choose to grade at a mid-way point in the course and then again at the end of the paper so as to be available for active participation in discussion and formative interaction in other weeks. Grading for participation is advocated by Earl and Cong (2011) on the grounds that students expect and appreciate receiving a participation grade. The Chinese students studying in a New Zealand context in Earl and Cong's small study, indicated that they approve of awarding grades for discussion participation, and that a grade is useful for encouragement, is an incentive to participate, is motivating, provides feedback, and reassures them that a "teacher's requirements" have been met (2011, p. 99). The authors conclude that since the students want a mark for discussion, they should receive one. However, we question whether providing a mark/grade for participating in an online discussion is the most pedagogically sound way to promote deep learning while meeting students' needs for rewards. For example, we suggest that encouragement and feedback can occur by interacting formatively with other learners in discussions; and propose that incentive and motivation can be intrinsic to discussions rather than being rewarded extrinsically (Forbes, 2005; Gikandi et al., 2011).

Other authors also take issue with grading participation. Hew and Cheung (2003) criticise the practice and suggest it encourages students merely to post just for the sake of showing the teacher they have done so (Hew & Cheung, 2003). Hewitt (2005), also questions the value of posting to be seen, or performative posting:

> Rather than focusing on progressive, sustained knowledge advancement, learners may feel that their primary objective is to simply participate in the conference and to be seen participating. Grading schemes that require students to contribute a certain number of notes each week may reinforce this view. (Hewitt, 2005, p. 584)

A number of critics therefore argue that grading participation in AOD weakens the potential for students to work as a learning community. According to Brookfield and Preskill (2012) for example:

> When discussion participation is graded it can easily undermine the quality of class exchanges, as the focus shifts away from developing shared understandings and toward making sure that individuals get full credit for what they say (p. 242).

In this way, the purpose of discussion is interpreted as meeting teachers' requirements, as students in Earl and Cong's (2011) study demonstrate. Garrison and Anderson (2003) highlight the student perspective, saying that:

> Omnipresent assessment may lead students to conclude that the discussion is a 'teacher tool' and not one which they may create and modify to meet their individual and group educational needs (p. 95)

Thus, Garrison and Anderson (2003) argue that such grading reduces student agency. This too links to the above argument about weakening potential online communities.

If participation is graded, students come to see that participation is about posting to be seen, to meet the requirements of the teacher, and to gain an individual grade. This is at the expense of interacting within a learning community and contributing to the learning of others. Thus:

> Systems based on extrinsic rewards quickly turn moral obligation into acts of self-interest, and could potentially destroy the open provision of knowledge in a community. (McLure Wasko & Faraj, 2000, p. 170)

An alternative approach is to leave discussion ungraded. However, teachers may be reluctant to remove all assessment on the grounds that this can render AOD peripheral (Brookfield & Preskill, 2005; Dennen, 2005; La Pointe, 2007). After all, as Garrison and Anderson (2003) recognise:

> Most students are …adults with much competition for their time, thus they are unlikely to participate in activities that are marginalized or viewed as supplemental to the course goals and assessment schema (p. 96)

Since assessment influences both how students spend their time and the type of learning taking place, the challenge is to assess in such a way as to encourage deep as opposed to surface approaches to learning (Arend, 2007). While grading for participation arguably encourages 'going through the motions' or posting just to satisfy teachers' requirements (Hew & Cheung, 2003), a solution gaining popularity is to devise a separate assessment task that is contingent upon discussion, while leaving the discussion itself ungraded. The contingent task can take the form of a reflective self assessment portfolio in which students audit, analyse and quote their own contributions to discussion in order to present evidence of meaningful participation and subsequent learning (Akyol & Garrison, 2008; Brookfield & Preskill, 2005; Garrison & Anderson, 2003; Jetton, 2003). For example, in one of her assignments, Liang requires her students to analyse their own discussion posts using the text analysis tools introduced in the course. With this assignment in mind, the students are

5.3 Assessment for Summative Purposes

In relation to assessment for summative purposes, the focus group tertiary teaching participants in Forbes (2012) commented that they found assessing online discussion to be challenging and contentious. Teachers reported difficulties with establishing criteria suited to this assessment, and wrestled with issues of weighting, objectivity, and manageability. The teachers felt that analysing online discussions for assessment purposes was a time consuming, labour-intensive task, ill supported by technical systems. They said it was extremely challenging to formulate useful and timely feedback for large numbers of students, with any level of individualisation or personalisation. Overall, teachers were divided on the value of assessing discussion. Some provided a summative weighting for discussion in order to motivate students, highlighting a perception among staff that if discussion wa not assessed then students would not bother to take part. Allocating a summative weighting to discussion thus rewarded students for prioritising this aspect of their work. One participant noted that

> When you start to assess discussion that's all very well because there's a motivation there for students to actually come online and do their thing because if you don't have that then they don't do it, traditionally, in my experience, they don't bother.

Others noted that,

> If there's absolutely no assessment part in it, quite often they just won't come in. And how do we know if they're lurking behind? How do we know that... they've agreed to do this, to become a community, as part of a community, and a community responsibility is to have some sort of a Presence.
>
> I give them 10% to motivate them, I figure if I'm asking them to do quite a bit of discussion and to really think about the readings, I think I should give them some credit.

Other teachers in Forbes's research explicitly reacted against the notion that students participated purely for marks, or that they should be rewarded for meeting this basic expectation. For example:

> I honestly do not believe that a student's engagement in a forum discussion has anything to do with a grade.

Several teachers felt that discussions functioned as tutorials, supportive of and preparatory for other assignments, rather than as assessment tasks. In some cases, discussions did not carry summative weightings, but were deemed both a compulsory requirement and a commitment to the community of learners. For example:

> It's a compulsory component. But I have found that having no marks attached hasn't actually altered the quality of what you get. You get people who are really into it, and if people are not

then and I will send them a private message saying ... because we are a community you've got an obligation to your colleagues really.

I tell them the discussions are not weighted but are attached to assignments, so if they do discussions these will help with assignments. I explain to them how the discussions link into the assignments, and of course the assignments have got weight but the discussions themselves don't. I say that the discussions aren't compulsory, but they help you with the assignments. I don't tell them not to do them. I reckon if they do the discussions online, this will come through in their assignments in terms of clarity and depth of thought.

Some teachers supported student learning via prompt and regular feedback, creating a formative and summative dimension to assessment. For example:

I think the assessed component supports the quality of discussion immensely because the students are continually aiming for the best grade. But really we treat it as a formative process as well so we are giving students feedback throughout, so out of those five assessed weeks, students are receiving a mark at the end of each week, and critical feedback which enables them to really improve the quality of their discussion.

Some teachers stated a preference for student self-assessment of discussion, indicating that if criteria were shared then student judgements of their own performance were likely to be fairly accurate:

What I do think however is that it is a good idea to get students to assess themselves, and give themselves a mark. I mean they know what the criteria are, they're given to them. If you used that totally, they'd probably end up with grades that were just a little tougher than if you'd given them yourself.

Some teachers experimented with negotiating criteria with students, along with student self-assessment, moderated by the teacher:

There is a certain amount of self assessment and peer assessment, and so they set the criteria so as a group, as a class, we work through that. I do final sort of tweaking but they are in control of the assessment themselves.

Some teachers said they chose to select some discussions for formal assessment, while leaving other discussions unassessed. In some cases, students were asked to self-select discussions for assessment, inviting them to appraise and nominate their own best work. Overall, the teachers regarded online discussion assessment as problematic and some admitted to changing their approach each year and experimenting with ways around the issues:

Sometimes I've assessed online discussion and sometimes I haven't, and I'm not convinced that it makes much difference at all in terms of the amount of contribution and the quality of it. I've done various things, and if you're going to put a 10% weighting on discussion, I mean well does it really matter if they do or they don't? I know I've spoken to others who say you either put 25% on it or you don't bother. I've come round to thinking that yes, that's correct. 10% doesn't mean anything.

One teacher shared a particular approach to assessing online discussion, combining elements of attendance and participation, preparation for assignments, and student reflections on discussion as an assessment task:

what we've done is we've said 'discussion is your proof of participation and attendance', but beyond that, we're not assessing the quality of your discussion. So, we've got other assessments. However, one of those assessments is write up a discussion. Write up a discussion. In other words, canvas what was said in a discussion, summarise what was said, highlight the main points, show your own thinking and your own response to the points raised, etc, etc, etc. So, there is assessment ON the discussion rather than the discussion being the assessment and that has been extremely useful. We also use that as a catch-up assessment task for students who, for one reason or another, miss a discussion.

5.4 Formative—Summative Tensions

Forbes's (2012) research revealed some formative summative assessment tensions. Some student participants reported that they preferred the online discussion component of a paper to carry a summative weighting, so that they could prioritise this work in relation to other course commitments. The students contended that discussion was a great deal of work and should be rewarded accordingly with a grade. For example, Jacqui explained that in her first year of study, she spent a great deal of time on online discussion and felt this time could have been spent on other assessment tasks. As she explained:

> the amount of time I spent was just completely unrealistic to the percentage of the mark that it was affecting so that made a really big difference for me.

This is in keeping with the views expressed by some teachers who agreed that a summative weighting is needed to motivate and reward students in relation to discussion. For example, according to staff in the first focus group:

> if there's absolutely no assessment part in it, quite often they just won't come in.
>
> they don't do it, traditionally, in my experience, they don't bother.

The student participants were divided on this issue, however, with some students disagreeing that discussion should carry a summative weighting, and instead expressing a preference for freedom to discuss in order to test ideas without fear of losing marks. For example, Don asserted:

> We need a place to test our ideas and theories with others, where we can make our mistakes with no pressure of marks being lost.

Like other students, Don went on to compare discussion to a tutorial on campus, which is not assessed summatively. In Sarah's words:

> since it is the equivalent of being in-class, I don't see that marks are even necessary.

Similarly, some teachers explained that they preferred to make discussion a compulsory task without any summative weighting, thus conveying an expectation that participation in online discussion was required, but not graded. Staff reacted against the notion that students should be rewarded for meeting a basic expectation.

And some staff too, preferred that the discussion be regarded as a site for preparation of other assignments in a paper, akin to a tutorial.

In summary, the tertiary students and teachers in Forbes's (2012) study reported some confusion about the balance between learning through discussion, and the use of discussion as a summative assessment task. Some students prioritised learning and testing of ideas, while other students regarded discussion as an assessment task and sought to allocate their time in accordance with the summative weighting of the task. While teachers highlighted the learning and formative potential of discussion, some considered it necessary to summatively assess discussion in order to motivate and reward students for the time and effort involved in contributing. However, other teachers and some students reiterated the notion of online discussion as a tutorial and argued that participation should be required and directed toward preparation for other assigned tasks, along with wider learning, exploration and professional preparation.

Within the literature, one strand of thought assumes that there is little choice but to grade student discussion in a university context (e.g. Arend, 2007; Dennen, 2005; Earl & Cong, 2011). For the most part, this is because the grading of discussion is deemed necessary in order to motivate students to participate. There is a need for further research to verify whether this is indeed the case. The assignment of grades to discussion is questioned by key commentators like Jacques and Salmon (2007), and Brookfield and Preskill (2005), with the former regarding this grading as a concern due to the attempt to "force" motivation or participation (Jacques & Salmon, 2007, p. 217). While in agreement with these concerns about debasing the quality of contributions, and promoting individual credit over the development of shared understandings, Brookfield and Preskill (2005) acknowledge the tension between grading discussion and shifting rewards away from discussion altogether. It is unrealistic and arguably unfair to expect participants to devote time and energy to discussion, if they are instead rewarded for work undertaken elsewhere while discussion is marginalised (Garrison & Anderson, 2003; LaPointe, 2007). However, Askell-Williams and Lawson (2005) acknowledge that the assessment of discussion can constrain students' participation and enjoyment of discussion.

A dilemma here concerns how to encourage time-poor students (and staff) to accord sufficient priority to learning through AOD, while promoting higher order thinking, deep learning and community; and discouraging a purely instrumental approach to summative assessment. This calls for a strategic approach to the motivation and assessment of discussion.

Philosophically, we argue that extrinsic motivation via grading is not the best model for tertiary students; and that the notion of discussion as a tutorial is more in keeping with the deep approach to learning we should strive for in higher education. Although extrinsic motivation may work in terms of getting students to attend or participate in discussion, it is not going to be effective in helping them to engage in anything beyond surface learning, and it will not promote commitment to their professional and learning communities.

The teachers in Forbes's (2012) study described discussion as a tutorial, characterised by formative interaction. Summing up and building upon their learning through AOD, students can present their work for summative assessment in another format—essay, presentation, or portfolio. Discussion is a process, and a secondary artifact should be submitted for summative assessment purposes (Ferdig & Roehler, 2003). This approach is supported by Garrison and Anderson (2003), who suggest that students produce a reflection piece incorporating illustrative quotations from discussion. Brookfield and Preskill (2005, p. 277) also advocate a "discussion audit" process whereby students analyse and summarise discussion to create a portfolio submission. In this way, students are empowered to produce their own evidence of learning, and assessment is congruent with the deep learning intended.

In summary, this chapter has considered key findings around presence for learning, with emphasis on participants' expectations of active participation and responsive communication, characterised by formative interaction. At issue in this section is the tension between assessment for summative and formative purposes. Ways of managing this tension are suggested, and the details of these approaches could be negotiated in the establishment of purpose and expectations as per section one.

5.5 Takeaway Tips

To promote deep learning strategically, AOD needs to be:

- an expectation and requirement, in keeping with the students' obligation to the learning community;
- subject to student reflection and self-assessment, in order to promote metacognition and deep approaches to learning;
- closely linked to other assessed work, complementing the discussion. In effect, the summative assessment tasks should be contingent upon commitment to AOD.

References

Arend, B. D. (2007). Course assessment practices and student learning strategies in online courses. *Journal of Asynchronous Learning Networks, 11*(4), 3–17.

Askell-Williams, H., & Lawson, M. J. (2005). Students' knowledge about the value of discussions for teaching and learning. *Social Psychology of Education, 8*(1), 83–115.

Akyol, Z., & Garrison, D. R. (2008). The development of a community of inquiry over time in an online course: Understanding the progression and integration of social, cognitive and teaching presence. *Journal of Asynchronous Learning Networks, 12*(3/4), 3–22.

Brookfield, S., & Preskill, S. (2005). *Discussions as a way of teaching: Tools and techniques for democratic classrooms* (2nd ed.). JosseyBass.

Brookfield, S. D., & Preskill, S. (2012). *Discussion as a way of teaching: Tools and techniques for democratic classrooms*. John Wiley & Sons.

Dennen, V. P. (2005). From message posting to learning dialogues: Factors affecting learner participation in asynchronous discussion. *Distance Education, 26*(1), 127–148.

Earl, K., & Cong, Y. (2011). Chinese international students' experience of studying online in New Zealand. *Waikato Journal of Education, 16*(1), 93–105.

Ellis, R. A., Goodyear, P., Calvo, R. A., & Prosser, M. (2008). Engineering students' conceptions of and approaches to learning through discussion in face-to-face and online contexts. *Learning and Instruction, 18*(3), 267–282.

Fauske, J., & Wade, S. E. (2003). Research to practice online: Conditions that foster democracy, community, and critical thinking in computer-mediated discussions. *Journal of Research on Technology in Education, 36*(2), 137–153.

Ferdig, R. E., & Roehler, L. R. (2003). Student uptake in electronic discussions: Examining online discourse in literacy preservice classrooms. *Journal of Research on Technology in Education, 36*(2), 119–136.

Forbes, D. (2005). Formative interaction in online classes. *International Journal of Design Sciences and Technology (Revue des Science et Techniques de la Conception). Special issue: eLearning Challenge, 12*(2), 83–93.

Forbes, D. L. (2012). *Footprints: Participant perspectives informing pedagogy for asynchronous online discussion in initial teacher education* (Doctoral dissertation, University of Waikato).

Forbes, D. (2015). Beyond lecture capture: Student-generated podcasts in teacher education. *Waikato Journal of Education, 20*(3). https://doi.org/10.15663/wje.v20i3.234

Garrison, D. R., & Anderson, T. (2003). *E-learning in the 21st century*. London, England: Routledge Falmer.

Gikandi, J. W., Morrow, D., & Davis, N. E. (2011). Online formative assessment in higher education: A review of the literature. *Computers & Education, 57*(4), 2333–2351. https://doi.org/10.1016/j.compedu.2011.06.004

Haythornthwaite, C., & Andrews, R. (2011). *E-learning theory and practice*. Sage Publications.

Hew, K. F., & Cheung, W. S. (2003). Evaluating the participation and quality of thinking of preservice teachers in an asynchronous online discussion environment: Part I. *International Journal of Instructional Media, 30*(3), 247.

Hewitt, J. (2005). Toward an understanding of how threads die in asynchronous computer conferences. *Journal of the Learning Sciences, 14*(4), 567–589.

Holmes, B., & Gardner, J. (2006). *E-learning: Concepts and practice*. Sage Publications.

Jacques, D., & Salmon, G. (2007). *Learning in groups: A handbook for face-to-face and online environments* (4th ed.). Routledge.

Jetton, T. L. (2003). Using computer-mediated discussion to facilitate preservice teachers' understanding of literacy assessment and instruction. *Journal of Research on Technology in Education, 36*(2), 171–191.

LaPointe, D. K. (2007). Pursuing interaction. In J. M. Spector (Ed.), *Finding your voice online: Stories told by experienced online educators* (pp. 83–103). Lawrence Erlbaum Associates Inc.

Locke, T. (2007). E-learning and the reshaping of rhetorical space. In R. Andrews & C. A. Haythornthwaite (Eds.), *The Sage handbook of e-learning research* (pp. 179–201). Sage Publications.

Loughran, J. (2006). *Developing a pedagogy of teacher education: Understanding teaching and learning about teaching*. Routledge.

McLure Wasko, M., & Faraj, S. (2000). "It is what one does": Why people participate and help others in electronic communities of practice. *The Journal of Strategic Information Systems, 9*(2–3), 155–173.

Chapter 6
Innovative Practices in Online Discussion

Abstract This chapter looks at creative approaches to discussion, with a focus on innovative content, ways of involving participants, and variations to online tools. We consider the integration of active and practical learning with AOD and provide specific examples of activities used in online classes. We advocate challenging students' thinking by allocating leadership roles and eliciting fresh perspectives; inviting guests to participate; and extending the use of a range of digital tools to enrich the discussion.

Joanna, a teaching and learning advisor, was showcasing digital learning tools to a group of teachers. During her demonstration, she happened to open an online discussion activity she had used for demonstration. The activity followed a single-answer discussion design, and a list of answers were posted by various students with minimal interactions among them. Upon seeing this rather plain display and the limited interactions, a couple of teachers began to voice their opinions that online discussions were old-fashioned and uninteresting as a teaching approach. This led to the questions: Is online discussion truly out of date? Can it still be used innovatively?

In chapter 4, we explored the integration of online discussions into teaching practices. Here in chapter 6, we aim to present a collection of innovative practices that we have found valuable in our teaching. These innovations encompass the content of online discussion, the involvement of discussion participants, and the use of diverse tools.

6.1 Content of Online Discussion

We have already discussed the design of online discussion starters to provoke thinking. Online discussions, however, do not need to be limited to what happens in the forum or online. Discussions can be used to facilitate other activities such as group work, fieldwork (e.g. Scanlan & Hancock, 2010), or virtual field experiences (e.g. Han, 2021). Discussion forums can also serve as a space for participants to express self-reflections, seek clarifications or verifications, and engage in ideas or interact with teammates for various online or offline activities (Forbes, et al., 2023).

Discussion forums can be created separately from the activity space, but we will use Wiki[1] in Moodle, a toolkit, as an example here to showcase the application of discussions. Wiki serves as versatile tools that not only support collaborative content creation among participants, but also offer a space named Comments for discussions directly associated with the collaborative task. As online discussion is the primary focus of our book, we will closely examine the discussions taking place in the Comments forum of a Wiki activity that Liang used in her Chinese reading and translation course.

A Wiki-based group translation activity was one of the online activities in Liang's course. Each group, consisting of a maximum of five students, was required to work collaboratively to translate one section of an English book into Chinese, and to give a brief presentation outlining the translation principles and strategies employed during the process. At the beginning of the activity, Wiki was introduced to the students and the students were instructed to use Wiki for all their translation-related work. Their editing process documented in Wiki was also counted for assessment purposes. During the translation, many students not only were actively involved in the editing process, but also left comments to each other using the Comments space. The following are three examples from their discussions:

1. Hi, 大家好，我做了一些关于cohesive flow的搜索。这个词的词义就是衔接，亦或者是局部衔接，句子清晰明了地衔接在一起，让读者可以毫无障碍地从一个句子流畅地读到下一个句子，所以我就把它的意思翻译成了"衔接流畅"。如果我翻译的这个意思有失偏颇，麻烦修改一下。

Translation

Hello, everyone! I did some research on the term "cohesive flow". It means 衔接 (cohesion) or 局部衔接 (partial cohesion). Here it refers to sentences being tightly connected, allowing readers to read fluently from one sentence to the next. In light of this, I translated it as "衔接流畅". If my translation is not accurate, please feel free to make any necessary corrections.

In this example, the student discussed her translation process, sharing insights into how she tackled the phrase "cohesive flow" by searching for its meaning and carefully considering its context. At the end, she sought help from her group members, inviting them to review and revise her translation output.

2. 还有一个点是，在我们中英翻译的时候，需要特别注意量词。

原文："It was created by six different writers, one of whom wrote the first sentence."

翻译软件的译文："这篇文章是由六个不同的作者创作的,其中的一个写了第一个句子。"

从这个翻译中，"六个作者" 和 "一个" 是错误的中文表达方式。我们知道,如果使用正确的中文量词去表达，应该是："六位作者" 和 "一位"。虽然英语中也有量词,比如"a piece of cake" 一块蛋糕和 "a cluster of trees" 一片树林,但是有些中文量词在英语中

---

[1] A wiki is a website in which the content is created collaboratively by a community.

6.1 Content of Online Discussion

是没有对应的表达方式的。例如,"一颗苹果","五栋楼房" 或者 "两支笔"。所以我们翻译时需要注意中文量词的使用~

我认为翻译过程是很有趣的,它涉及到不同语言和文化之间的交流和理解。我十分享受这个过程!

Translation

Another aspect to consider when we translate from English to Chinese is that we need to pay special attention to measure words.

Original text: "It was created by six different writers, one of whom wrote the first sentence."

The Chinese translation provided by the software: "这篇文章是由六个不同的作者创作的,其中的一个写了第一个句子。"

In this translation, "六个作者" (six authors) and "一个" (one) are incorrect Chinese expressions. We know that if the correct Chinese measure word is used, it should be: "六位作者" (six authors) and "一位" (one). Although English uses measure words in phrases like "a piece of cake" and "a cluster of trees", some Chinese measure words do not have direct equivalents in English. For example, "一颗苹果" (one apple), "五栋楼房" (five buildings), or "两支笔" (two pens). So it is important to pay attention to the appropriate usage of Chinese measure words during translation ~

I find the translation process very interesting, as it involves the interaction and interpretation between different languages and cultures. I thoroughly enjoy the process!

Example 2 comprises a more extensive discussion. The incorrect translation of the software prompted the student to reflect on the different use of measure words in Chinese and English. In order to support her idea, the student provided a couple of examples from both languages. She also expressed her positive attitude towards the translation process, viewing it as an interactive and interpretive exchange between diverse languages and cultures.

3. 感谢大家的翻译和贡献,大家的评论都十分的有用!! 😵

在我去翻译和分析这个文章时,我对比了一些我的翻译和翻译软件的内容,我是碰到了一些疑惑的。

比如这句话 "When you create cohesive flow"

用软件翻译出来的内容是:当您创建有凝聚力的流程时

而我的个人翻译是:当你书写的内容衔接流畅时

这两句翻译的对比,让我感受到了翻译软件在翻译的过程中过于逐字逐句,导致翻译结果模式单一,很生硬。因此,我们在后期的校对和修改时还是得注意上下文内容,让翻译内容更加有逻辑和容易理解。

Translation

Thank you for your translations and contributions. The comments from everyone have been incredibly helpful!! 😵

During the process of translating and analysing this article, when I compared some of my translations with those generated by the translation software, I was sometimes puzzled.

For example, the words "When you create cohesive flow"

The software's translation is: 当您创建有凝聚力的流程时 (when you create cohesive processes)

While my translation reads: 当你书写的内容衔接流畅时

Comparing these two translations made me realise that the translation software often provides word-for-word translation, resulting in a literal and straightforward translation. Therefore, during the proofreading and revision stage it becomes crucial to consider the context to make the translated content more logical and easier to understand.

Example 3 was posted near the end of the translation activity, so the student started her post by acknowledging the valuable contributions of her peers. She then focused on the shortcomings of the translation software by comparing its output and her own translation. Additionally, she explored the reasons behind the software's rigid translation and suggested a potential solution to address the problem.

We can see from the above three examples that by means of discussions these students checked the accuracy of their own translation output, highlighted the key difference between the source and target language, and pointed out the drawback of the translation software. At the same time, they actively built up interpersonal connections with their group members by inviting others' feedback, expressing their own feelings, and offering appreciation for their peers' contributions. In this case, learning occurs in two distinct settings: during the translation and editing process itself and during the interaction between the students. Online discussions create the opportunity for participants to explicitly articulate their thoughts and reflections on their task, no matter if it is online or offline, and allow their peers to read and respond to their ideas, cultivating a team spirit as they move forward together. In these examples, it can be seen that online discussions can play a vital role in enhancing the overall learning experience.

6.2 Involvement of Discussion Participants

Innovations relating to discussion participants revolve around the change of student participation patterns, the involvement of students in leading discussions, resource building and module summary, and the negotiation of discussion guidelines with students. All three approaches will be further discussed under the section student roles. The underlying idea of all three approaches is to empower students to take on leadership roles in their own learning. Alongside students and teachers, the inclusion of a third party in asynchronous online discussions can further enhance and expand upon these innovative approaches. This will be tackled under the section guest lecturers and stakeholders.

6.2.1 Student Roles

An alternative, fun option to participate in discussions is role play, which enhances the connection between learning and play. As Bonk and Khoo (2014) argue, "we

6.2 Involvement of Discussion Participants

play to learn" (p. 117). Scripted roles have been suggested in the literature for the benefits of fostering more equitable discussions (Cacciamani et al., 2019; Hambacher et al., 2018; Brookfield & Preskill, 2005), facilitating connections between group member (Cacciamani et al., 2019; Hambacher et al., 2018; Olesova et al., 2016), promoting novel ideas and deep learning (Hambacher et al., 2018; Olesova et al., 2016), and exposing diverse approaches to contribute to group talks (Brookfield & Preskill, 2005). Research in this area involves the assignment of different roles to students, such as *starter*, *skeptic* and *wrapper* in Olesoba et al. (2016); *first responder*, *connector* and *synthesizer* in Hambacher et al. (2018); *social tutor*, *synthesizer*, *sceptic* and *concept mapper* in Cacciamani et al. (2019); and *problem, dilemma, or theme poser*, *reflective analyst*, and *scrounger* in Brookfield and Preskill (2005).

Unlike most studies, a broader range of roles from Salmon (2000) (see Table 6.1) are adapted in Dianne and Liang's courses, and multiple students are assigned the same roles in larger groups. We aimed to distribute various responsibilities of online teachers into separate roles and allocate them to individual students. We recognise the importance of teacher presence as highlighted in chapter 4, but when it is possible, we use a role play approach to gradually decrease the need for teacher involvement in discussions, placing control in the hands of students. As teachers, we still actively monitor the discussion, but our expectation is that students will independently take on their assigned roles and work collaboratively to lead and moderate discussions. At the same time, by assigning students roles, we aim to interrupt students' habitual patterns of participation and open up alternative perspectives for their contributions. As student leadership is expected in role play activities, role play is more suitable to be introduced in the second half of the course, after students become familiar with discussions and develop rapport with their team members.

Teachers can assign roles to individual students to engage them in discussions or hand over the facilitator role to students. Nicola negotiated a schedule with her students at the start of the year, allocating each week to a different student, who would be responsible for summarising the reading material, posing discussion questions, and concluding the discussion at the end of the week.

Besides individual students, roles can also be allocated to different teams to prepare for and conclude discussions. 'Module tutor' is a role introduced in Liang's large hybrid class and teams of 3–5 students are assigned as module tutors for each module. As tutors, students are responsible for sharing a short resource of any format (e.g. texts, images, audios or videos) relating to the module and presenting the key points of their module discussion using a ppt slide, a question, a quote and an image. Both resources and summaries are shared in the Moodle Glossary platform for the entire class. As students are often allocated to different discussion groups in a large class, this activity not only promotes module tutors' self-study by encouraging them to identify the key points of their group discussions but also facilitates cross-group learning by sharing ideas from each group's discussion. In addition, the shared work helps teachers to gauge the students' understanding of the module and enriches the course resources for both current and future students.

Another approach to sharing power with students is to involve students in the discussion management. Dianne in her study (Forbes, 2015) negotiated discussion

Table 6.1 Online discussion roles and descriptions

Roles	Descriptions
Discussion leader	The role of the discussion leader is to ask questions, clarify understanding, and generally make sure the discussion keeps rolling along in a productive way. As the leader, your job is to make sure the questions get answered and your group is on task!
Literary giant	You have a really good grasp of the current literature. You will also want to help your group members make connections between the reading and their presented examples by asking them some questions
Story teller	You love to tell stories or present case studies to make the theory or concepts come alive and relevant for the other members of your group
Devil's advocate	You argue against a cause or position for the sake of argument or to determine the validity of the cause or position. Often you raise the worse case scenario even though you might not believe it to be the case. Because you keep challenging the group they do not always like your constant demands for answers but you do not give up!
Eternal optimist	You always seem to look on the bright side of any suggestions. "Of course we can do it, nothing will get in our way." Obstacles are just minor irritations to be dealt with so that you can move on to bigger and better things. In the discussion you try to put a good light on anything that looks vaguely negative
Eternal pessimist	You always seem to look on the dark side of any suggestions. "Well of course it is never going to work is it!" There are always one hundred and one reasons you can come up with to put a dampener on the discussion. Any good ideas must be squashed immediately!
Balanced fence-sitter	You aim for balance in all expressions of views. It might be considered that you 'sit on the fence', as you strive to see both sides of any issue or debate
Summariser	The role of the summariser is to pull together different ideas and opinions and show the connections between the different comments made by group members. Every few days you have a habit of wrapping up the discussion by making some statements about the trends, key points, main ideas, and statements to remember in the discussion
Equity adviser	You are always keen to ensure that everybody is able to reach their potential and people feel included in the discussion activity even though they may appear to be a little anxious about joining in. Issues of diversity are paramount in your thinking and you want people's voices to be heard. You remind people that this is not a monocultural society in which we live and we have to be inclusive

guidelines with her teacher education students in two discussion-driven Moodle courses. The guidelines developed from her doctoral research were proposed to initiate the conversation and an anonymous discussion forum was used to reduce student concern and increase their level of engagement. Students were invited to consider "the purpose, expectations, assessment and suggestions" (p. 88) relating to asynchronous online discussion. Through this negotiation process, several key themes emerged. Firstly, students expressed their concerns about the precision and length of postings. Secondly, they expected their peers to be responsive by providing relevant contributions and by avoiding overlooking or duplicating posts. Additionally, students valued respect when challenging ideas and inclusivity when selecting posts to respond to. These suggestions were included in the discussion guidelines for future students. The process of negotiation enabled students to gain valuable insights from the perspective of teachers and allowed teachers to hear student voices and to receive fresh input for the development of the course.

6.2.2 Guest Lecturers and Stakeholders

Various roles and responsibilities have been discussed above with regard to student participation. While students are the primary participants, asynchronous online discussions offer the advantage of involving a third party to further enrich the conversations. Guest lecturers, in particular, are an excellent source of knowledge. Inviting stakeholders from different walks of life can also bring a unique perspective to discussions, expanding the conversation beyond the walls of the university.

Involving guest lecturers into online discussion can infuse forums with new insights, alternative perspectives, and a welcome change of pace (Bender, 2012). The affordance of e-learning tools and the flexibility of online learning makes it easier to invite guest speakers, without incurring the travel and accommodation expenses of on-campus visits (Bender, 2012). Additionally, guest lecturers can contribute to the asynchronous discussions on their own schedule or share pre-recorded videos with the class if they are unable to attend synchronous sessions. Dianne, Nicola and Liang have all invited guest lecturers to join their online courses and their students greatly appreciated and valued the insights and contributions of these guests.

Dianne and Nicola have found librarians particularly helpful in information-coaching roles within AOD. When students are undertaking research, engaging with library staff in discussion enables them to interact over an extended period with information experts who can provide timely support. In recent discussions, librarians have shared resources to help with keywords and searches and have helped undergraduate students with common challenges related to research and writing, including how to determine the quality of sources, how to take notes, paraphrase, synthesise and reference their work. Engaging with a librarian in online discussion raises students' awareness of the valuable services the library provides and empowers them to seek help from librarians in the future.

Liang delivers a reading and translation course tailored for Chinese students studying in a New Zealand university. While both Liang and another lecturer have extensive knowledge and years of experience in applied linguistics and translation, Liang seeks to enhance the course by incorporating the latest insights from China. To achieve this, she invited an experienced lecturer from a Chinese university to discuss the development of translation in China. The talk was in the format of an interview and pre-recorded due to the time difference and scheduling constraints. Questions for the interview were gathered from both teachers and students beforehand using an anonymous discussion forum. The video was then posted on Moodle for students to watch and discuss.

When inviting guest lecturers, an issue that may possibly arise is the payment expectation. As guest lecturers can come from a different context, it is important to consider this on a case-by-case basis. Some may offer their services for free, while others may expect payment, an exchange of teaching or other forms of reciprocity.

Apart from guest lecturers, guests from a professional field can also be a valuable asset to discussions, as these people will be colleagues, clients or stakeholders of our students in their future workplaces. Forbes and Ipsen (2004) included the voices of middle school pupils into the discussion of their teacher education students. The pupils' first-hand examples and personalised understandings from their classroom experiences challenged the student teachers' preconceptions. The conversations with pupils help student teachers to learn to listen to children's voices and to gain a better understanding of the capabilities and needs of their future students. Nicola often includes links to authors, illustrators, and librarians talking about their work in her children's literature classes to give her students insights into the world of practitioners.

6.3 Use of Diverse Tools

In addition to creative content and innovative participation, the emergence of various tools affords new teaching practices regarding online discussions. In this section, we will introduce three tools, Perusall, ChatGPT and AntConC, and discuss their affordances in terms of participant collaboration, content development, and efficient conclusion production.

Perusall is a free collaborative e-reading tool (Clarke, 2021), which facilitates learner-content, learner-teacher and learner-learner interactions, the three types of interactions in online classrooms (Moore, 1989). The interactions on Perusall, as reading-based online discussions, are asynchronous. With the help of Perusall, students are able to work in the "anchored environments" (Gao, et al., 2013, p. 476) to engage with the assigned reading, their teachers and peers by highlighting and annotating the texts with their own thoughts, questions and responses.

Perusall is also an effective tool with functions such as upvoting, grouping, and automatic marking. Upvoting is a quick and easy way to express one's support of an idea and to indicate one's social presence online. Grouping is especially useful for larger classes as it helps to avoid overwhelming students with too much information. The automatic marking system built into Perusall not only saves teachers' time but also motivates student contribution. Students can receive their score immediately after each contribution. Adams and Wilson (2020) found that the use of Perusall increased both text interaction and peer interaction in their study, which potentially led to community growth and deeper learning. A Perusall activity will be introduced following the introduction of ChatGPT, as the activity combines the use of Perusall and ChatGPT.

ChatGPT, recently launched by OpenAI, is a large language model (van Dis et al., 2023) and a highly sophisticated chatbot (Lund & Wang, 2023). It is able to interpret

6.3 Use of Diverse Tools

user requests and generate appropriate responses in human-like texts (Kasneci et al., 2023). It has the potential to create teaching materials but at the same time it carries the risk of producing inaccurate or fake information (Lo, 2023). As a user-friendly tool, it has gained enormous attention immediately after its release. Both Dianne and Liang have incorporated ChatGPT into their discussion design to foster learning about the course content and enhance digital literacy skills. Dianne prompted it to write a discussion starter. Liang created a specific reading material for her Perusall activity using a sequence of questions. Students' response has been positive as the activity was frequently mentioned in subsequent discussions and their assignments.

Liang planned to utilise Perusall, the social reading platform, to introduce interpersonal interaction strategies in written academic discourse. Ideally students should engage with one piece of reading material but the broad coverage of interpersonal interaction strategies makes it challenging to find suitable readings. To address this issue, Liang decided to collaborate with ChatGPT to create a tailored resource for the particular focus. As ChatGPT is a new tool, the created resource also provided an opportunity for students to become aware of its limitations.

Liang started with a general question asking ChatGPT what interpersonal interaction referred to in academic discourse and then prompted ChatGPT to suggest the frameworks of interpersonal interaction. ChatGPT responded by presenting three popular frameworks in the field. Liang then asked for detailed information including categories, language examples and references for each framework and requested ChatGPT to analyse a short discussion post employing each framework. The human-chatbot conversation ended with a comparison of different frameworks. Liang attempted a couple of times to prompt her desired answers and the final version of the generated resource beautifully covered all three important frameworks with a total of 3,758 words, the appropriate length for one-week reading-based discussion.

The generated reading was uploaded to Perusall. Liang highlighted sections of the text to add notes, ask questions and make comments. The question–answer format of the reading generated from ChatGPT lacked cohesion and coherence due to the absence of introduction, conclusion and transitions between each question, which could potentially hinder students' comprehension. Additionally, the text contains false information and misleading results of analysis. These limitations were compensated by the annotation function in Perusall. Introduction, conclusion and transitions were added as Perusall annotations where necessary. Sections were highlighted to prompt students to identify, discuss and correct the distorted information as well as expand upon the content. Students were also invited to evaluate ChatGPT and give suggestions to ChatGPT users at the end of this activity.

Liang's teaching design combined the strengths of ChatGPT and Perusall. With the help of ChatGPT, a customised reading material was effectively created through a series of questions. The distorted information generated by ChatGPT offers students a learning opportunity to assess the validity/authenticity of information, a crucial skill in today's information-driven world. The annotation function of Perusall allows teachers to improve the reading experience by incorporating background information, transitions and conclusions into the question–answer-based reading. More importantly, Perusall allows teachers and other experts in the field to "review, validate and explain" (Kasneci et al., 2023, p. 5) alongside the AI-generated information before presenting the information to the students, learners in the field.

ChatGPT facilitates discussion preparation, Perusall enhances the experience during the discussion, and AntConc is a tool that sums up the discussion. Summarisation of discussions is crucial for learning but the workload can be daunting as discussions of a larger class or over a longer time tend to be excessively lengthy. To streamline this process, Liang utilised the keyword function and collocate function in AntConC (https://www.laurenceanthony.net/software/antconc/), a free, simple and user-friendly corpus analysis toolkit (Anthony, 2022). Given that online discussions are primarily conducted through written texts (Fear & Erikson-Brown, 2014), the discussion posts for each module can be treated as a corpus and analysed using AntConC for efficient identification of key points.

AntConC can be downloaded from its website and the installation is straightforward. In order to create a corpus of discussion posts, all the discussion posts of a specific module need to be firstly exported into a Text document. Then run AntConC and choose "Create Quick Corpus" from the file menu to import the Text document. Now, the discussion post corpus can be seen under "Target Corpus". To generate the keywords (i.e. words that appear unusually frequent) from the target corpus, a reference corpus is needed for comparison. A pre-built reference corpus can be chosen from the default corpus library by choosing "Open Corpus Manager" under the file menu. The British English 2006 corpus (BE06) is suggested for New Zealand users as British English is commonly used in New Zealand. The last step is to click on the "Keyword" tab and "Start" button. A keyword list with rank, frequency, range and keyness will be displayed.

Figure 6.1 presents the keyword results of a discussion on Digital Learning in the Press. We can see from the top 10 keywords that the discussion in general tends to focus more on *learning* (Rank 1) and *students* (Rank 4) than on *teaching* (Rank 10) and *teachers* (Rank 9). *Covid*, the pandemic (Rank 6) is another popular theme at the time of the discussion. By clicking any one of these words, we can learn more details. For example, Fig. 6.2 shows the sentence contexts of *technology*, particularly *digital technology*. Students have already talked about the *use, acceptance, availability, role* and *understanding* of digital technology.

In this chapter, we have explored several innovative practices in online discussions with regard to the content, participant involvement and the utilisation of various tools. Online discussions can serve as standalone activities or as facilitators for other online or offline endeavours. When it comes to discussion participants, particularly students, they can assume diverse roles to contribute to the forum, prepare for or summarise discussions, or suggest discussion guidelines. Additionally, inviting guest lecturers and stakeholders to participate can bring valuable insights to the forum. By leveraging different tools like Perusall, ChatGPT and AntConC, the content of online discussions can be further enriched, the overall experience enhanced, and the supervision of discussions reinforced.

6.5 Takeaway Tips

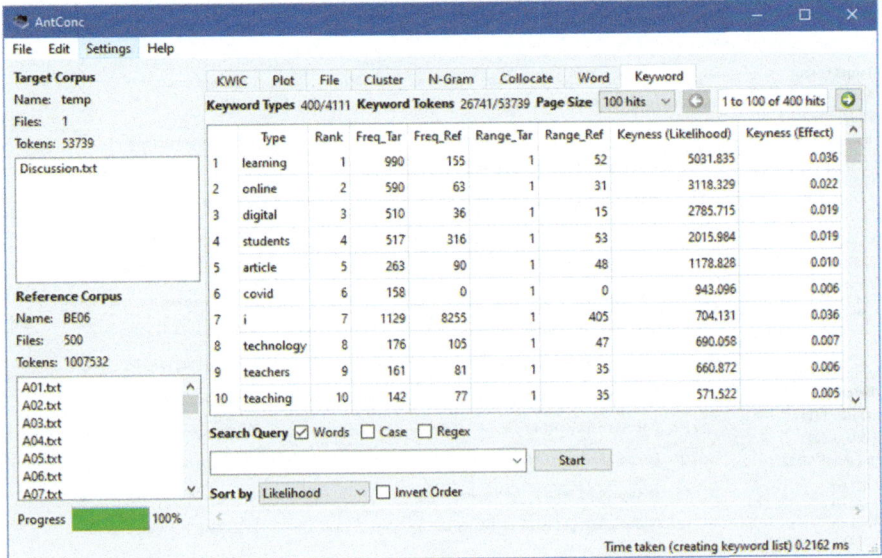

Fig. 6.1 The keyword results of a discussion on digital learning in the press

6.4 Return to Vignette

Now let's return to the question asked at the start of this chapter: Is online discussion truly out of date? The answer is clear. Instead of putting an end to online communication, we, as educators, can explore various methods to enrich our students' online interaction, supporting student–student and teacher-student scaffolding experiences. Joy accompanies us on our journey of exploration.

6.5 Takeaway Tips

Online discussions offer diverse opportunities for teaching and learning. Teachers can adopt an innovative approach by focusing on the following three key aspects:

- Enriching the content of discussions: Teachers can enhance the discussions by integrating other online or offline activities, such as group work, fieldwork or virtual reality activities. This approach broadens the scope of the discussions and provides students with a more comprehensive learning experience.
- Involving different insights in discussions: To foster a rich and diverse discussion, teachers can create space for students to take different roles in preparation, active participation, summarisation and discussion management. Moreover, inviting external parties like guest lecturers or stakeholders can bring unique insights to discussions.

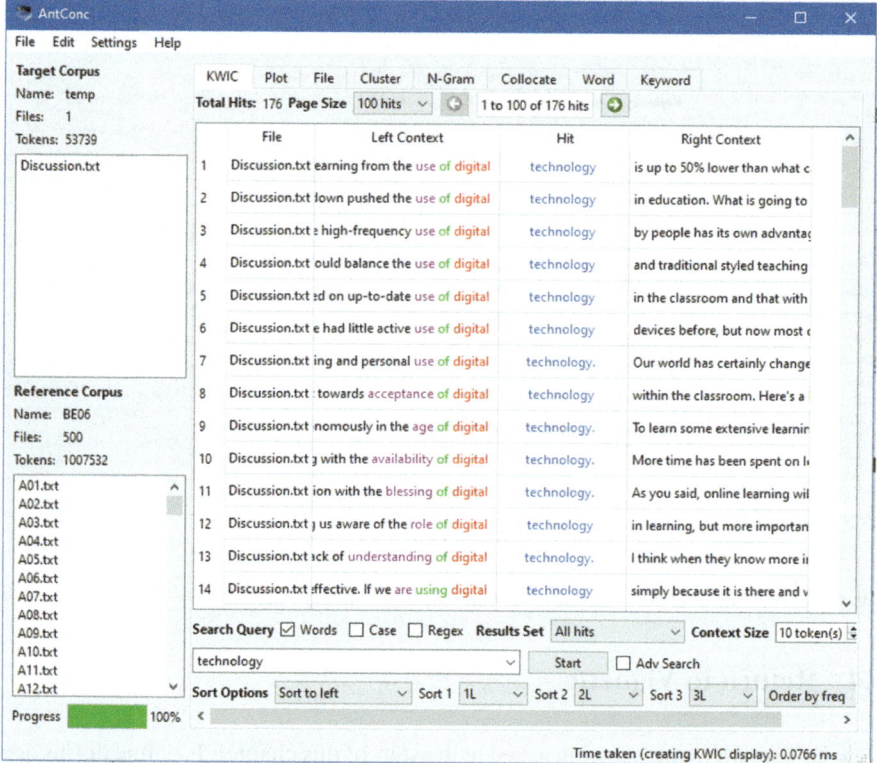

Fig. 6.2 The sentence contexts of *technology*

- Enhancing the experience of discussions: Applying various tools and technologies can significantly improve the overall experience of online discussions. Tools like ChatGPT, Perusalls and AntConC can contribute to material compilation, facilitating human-content and human–human interactions, and highlighting key points of discussions. By leveraging these tools, teachers can create engaging and interactive discussions and promote deeper learning.

Teachers can consider the above three aspects to create their own enriching and engaging learning environment that benefits both students and educators.

References

Adams, B., & Wilson, N. S. (2020). Building community in asynchronouns online higher education courses through collaborative annotation. *Journal of Educational Technology, 49*(2), 250–261. https://doi.org/10.1177/0047239520946422

References

Anthony, L. (2022). *AntConc*. In (Version Version 4.2.0) [Computer Software]. Waseda University. https://www.laurenceanthony.net/software

Bender, T. (2012). *Discussion-Based Online Teaching to Enhance Student Learning: Theory, Practice and Assessment*. Stylus Publishing, LLC. http://ebookcentral.proquest.com/lib/waikato/detail.action?docID=987038

Bonk, C. J., & Khoo, E. G. L. (2014). *Adding some TEC-variety: 100+activities for motivating and retaining learners online*. Open World Books. https://hdl.handle.net/10289/8787

Brookfield, S. D., & Preskill, S. (2005). *Discussion As a Way of Teaching: Tools and Techniques for Democratic Classrooms*. John Wiley & Sons, Incorporated. http://ebookcentral.proquest.com/lib/waikato/detail.action?docID=700322

Cacciamani, S., Cesareni, D., Perrucci, V., Balboni, G., & Khanlari, A. (2019). Effects of a social tutor on participation, sense of community and learning in online university courses. *British Journal of Educational Technology, 50*(4), 1771–1784. https://doi.org/10.1111/bjet.12656

Clarke, A. J. (2021). Perusall: Social learning platform for reading and annotating (perusall LLC, perusall.com). *Journal of political science education, 17*(1), 149–154. https://doi.org/10.1080/15512169.2019.1649151

Fear, W. J., & Erikson-Brown, A. (2014). Good quality discussion is necessary but not sufficient in asynchronous tuition: A brief narrative review of the literature. *Journal of asynchronous learning networks JALN, 18*(2), 21. https://doi.org/10.24059/olj.v18i2.399

Forbes, D., & Ipsen, S. (2004). 'It's like something in my perncilcase': Student teachers learning through ICT with digital kids. *Computers in New Zealand Schools, 16*(3), 49–53.

Forbes, D. (2015). Legacies of learning: Negotiating guidelines for online discussion. In N. Wright & D. Forbes (Eds.), *Digital smarts: Enhancing learning & teaching* (pp. 82–103). Wilf Malcolm Institute of Educational Research.

Forbes, D., Gedera, D., Brown, C., Hartnett, M., & Datt, A. (2023). Practical learning in hybrid environments: Can remote learning be active, authentic, and real? *Distance Education, 44*(2), 362–379. https://doi.org/10.1080/01587919.2023.2198487

Gao, F., Zhang, T., & Franklin, T. (2013). Designing asynchronous online discussion environments: Recent progress and possible future directions: Designing asynchronous discussion environments. *British Journal of Educational Technology, 44*(3), 469–483. https://doi.org/10.1111/j.1467-8535.2012.01330.x

Hambacher, E., Ginn, K., & Slater, K. (2018). Letting students lead: Preservice teachers' experiences of learning in online discussions. *Journal of Digital Learning in Teacher Education, 34*(3), 151–165. https://doi.org/10.1080/21532974.2018.1453893

Han, I. (2021). Immersive virtual field trips and elementary students' perceptions. *British Journal of Educational Technology, 52*(1), 179–195. https://doi.org/10.1111/bjet.12946

Kasneci, E., Sessler, K., Küchemann, S., Bannert, M., Dementieva, D., Fischer, F., Gasser, U., Groh, G., Günnemann, S., Hüllermeier, E., Krusche, S., Kutyniok, G., Michaeli, T., Nerdel, C., Pfeffer, J., Poquet, O., Sailer, M., Schmidt, A., Seidel, T., & Kasneci, G. (2023). ChatGPT for good? On opportunities and challenges of large language models for education. *Learning and Individual Differences, 103*, 102274. https://doi.org/10.1016/j.lindif.2023.102274

Lo, C. K. (2023). What is the impact of ChatGPT on education? A rapid review of the literature. *Education Sciences, 13*(4), 410. https://doi.org/10.3390/educsci13040410

Lund, B. D., & Wang, T. (2023). Chatting about ChatGPT: How may AI and GPT impact academia and libraries? *Library Hi Tech News, 40*(3), 26–29. https://doi.org/10.1108/LHTN-01-2023-0009

Moore, M. G. (1989). Editorial: Three types of interaction. *The American Journal of Distance Education, 3*(2), 1–7. https://doi.org/10.1080/08923648909526659

Olesova, L., Slavin, M., & Lim, J. (2016). Exploring the effect of scripted roles on cognitive presence in asynchronous online discussions. *Online learning (Newburyport, Mass.), 20*(4), 34–53. https://doi.org/10.24059/olj.v20i4.1058

Scanlan, J. N., & Hancock, N. (2010). Online discussions develop students' clinical reasoning skills during fieldwork. *Australian Occupational Therapy Journal, 57*(6), 401–408. https://doi.org/10.1111/j.1440-1630.2010.00883.x

van Dis, E. A. M., Bollen, J., Zuidema, W., van Rooij, R., & Bockting, C. L. (2023). ChatGPT: Five priorities for research. *Nature (london), 614*(7947), 224–226. https://doi.org/10.1038/d41586-023-00288-7

Chapter 7
The Future of Online Discussion

Abstract In this final chapter we bring together the major themes we have traversed in this book about Asynchronous Online Discussion (AOD), distilling key ideas and advice for using this online educational tool to its full potential.

Throughout this text, we have shared a range of stories, perspectives, and experiences. Starting with our own teaching philosophies and practices, across disciplines, and with students at various stages of study (undergraduate and postgraduate), we have highlighted the unique affordances of AOD for in-depth thinking and reflection. Fundamentally, our combined expertise in language and learning design has underpinned this text.

From the outset of this volume, there has been an emphasis on student voice and leadership, recognising the importance of peer interactions and learning as a community. Our thinking has been informed by seminal work like the Community of Inquiry framework (Garrison et al, 1999), and Ngā Hau e Whā o Tāwhirimātea (Rātima et al., 2022).

Our intent has been to delve into the complexities of learning through AOD—to analyse, unpack, and deconstruct it to unravel its inner workings. We have paid attention to the characteristics of AOD when it is effective for learning, but also crucially we have examined the limitations of ineffective discussion: when AOD is stilted, stale, and unsatisfying.

What has emerged has a practical simplicity, with tips for teachers and students alike, intended to help with the design of online discussion, and with commencing, sustaining, and concluding rich and satisfying interactions within AOD. We have distilled our discussion with tips at the end of each chapter.

Chapter 1 set the scene by outlining some of our experiences with AOD, anchoring AOD in the traditions of dialogic education and open and distributed learning. We established that, at its best, AOD can be inclusive, flexible, characterised by careful thinking and revisiting of persistent text, promoting reflection and deep learning over time. We acknowledged that these potential benefits of AOD are affordances that may not always be realised in practice. The challenge we set ourselves was to explore conditions under which AOD can be engaging and powerful for learning.

© The Author(s), under exclusive license to Springer Nature Singapore Pte Ltd. 2024
D. Forbes et al., *Designing Discussion for Online and Blended Courses*,
SpringerBriefs in Open and Distance Education,
https://doi.org/10.1007/978-981-97-6196-8_7

Chapter 2 focused on designing for diversity, as we recognise that there is no single approach to AOD, and that one size does not fit all. We highlighted the place of AOD outside of academia, acknowledging that learning in practice-oriented contexts also benefits from sharing of experiences, examples and challenges. Students can gather in a discussion forum to share the practical work they have experienced outside of the online class. Where students can benefit from community, AOD has a place. We highlighted and engaged with a framework for culturally responsive pedagogy, applying concepts of community, connection, care, and expertise to AOD. We proposed practical ways to offer students choices, in accordance with Universal Design for Learning (UDL).

Chapter 3 provided guidance for students learning through online discussion, addressing key concerns including sources of anxiety and confusion that are commonly experienced by students. We offered guidance to students to clarify the purpose and expectations of AOD, advised on the language of AOD, and on time management.

Parallel to this, chapter 4 provided similar guidance for teachers to enhance pedagogy and practice in AOD. Practicalities included how to stimulate, intervene and summarise in AOD to sustain productive learning dialogues. Variables around group size, specific pedagogical strategies, and teacher workload were outlined in this chapter.

The commonalities in the teaching and learning roles relate to the importance of crafting contributions that develop and sustain community, so that partners in discussion are acknowledged, while ideas are challenged, and new knowledge is built. Hurdles for students and teachers alike include the need to overcome paralysis when discussion stalls, how to balance active contributions with leaving space for others, and the ever-present realities of managing workload.

Chapter 5 tackled the contentious issue of assessing AOD, highlighting tensions between using discussion for teaching and learning (formative), as opposed to grading discussion summatively. To balance these tensions, we suggest an approach to assessment that promotes discussion as an obligation to a community of learners, while rewarding students' commitment and linking to wider assignments.

Chapter 6 canvased innovative approaches to AOD, demonstrating that the discussion forum is not merely a platform for online communication but also functions as an interaction hub for various online and offline activities. During online discussions, students can be empowered by taking on different roles, negotiating discussion guidelines and interacting with invited guest experts. The integration of a range of tools and technologies is suggested in order to take AOD into the future.

This final chapter (chapter 7) looks back at where we have been and dares to look forward to future possibilities. Some of these future-opportunities were foreshadowed in chapter 6, as the future is very much upon us. With time, what is innovative now will swiftly become commonplace, or may be relegated to history, and replaced by new tools, techniques, and pedagogies. It has been our contention from the beginning, however, that AOD should not be consigned to the past, due to the persistent value highlighted throughout this volume.

7.1 Ideas for Future Directions

Having presented recent research concerning the power of AOD in online education, we are in a position to point to future possibilities for research in this field. We can see, for example, that there is an expansive possibility for exploring the affordances of AOD to cater to the needs of diverse students, and diverse contexts. With the emergence of AI, we also see the potential for research focused on embracing AI as a discussion partner in AODs.

The work we have presented is contextualised in the experiences of the authors and students of a single institution in the main. We acknowledge the affordances of the rich and in-depth accumulation of experience which this has resulted in, and also the need for these findings to be explored across educational contexts. In particular, there are a range of tensions and challenges to explore, including the following:

- Tensions between expectations of diverse parties
- Establishing ground rules vs. evolving guidelines
- Active presence vs. wait time
- Formative vs. summative assessment
- Balancing teacher and student leadership

To guide future questions for exploration we suggest the following:

- How do participants view and experience AOD?
- What style of language is best suited to the context?
- What degree of active presence is best suited to the learning and teaching context?
- What is the purpose of assessment of AOD?
- How will the participants work together?

There are takeaway messages for both tertiary students and tertiary teachers from this text in relation to the possibilities of AOD in online learning. We hope the text is useful to tertiary teachers and to students, striving to engage in AOD as part of online and blended courses. We hope our attention to AOD reminds tertiary teachers that there is more to online learning than recorded lectures or synchronous videoconferencing.

To students, our message is to check out chapter 3 for insights into questioning, negotiated, participating and leading in AOD. Our advice is to approach discussion as a learning opportunity and to be open to changing your thinking on the basis of new evidence that evolves through discussion.

To tertiary teachers, we urge you to recognise the value of AOD as a site for classroom community and knowledge construction. Our message is that AOD can be inclusive, flexible, and ongoing, affording time to reflect and learn in depth. We have emphasised the need to be clear about the purpose of AOD and the expectations of students and staff alike. We encourage you to balance your own presence and engagement in discussion with invitation to students to lead. We hope you will actively consult with students, share ideas with colleagues, and experiment with different approaches to online discussion to keep the pedagogy alive.

To leaders in tertiary contexts, we encourage you to promote and adequately resource AOD, as it aligns with commonly agreed organisational values associated with nurturing community, supporting students, and enabling rich and flexible learning opportunities in diverse communities

We invite readers to trial the ideas, and to build upon them in the spirit of dialogic education that is the foundation of our scholarship. We look forward to engaging with readers who want to share further experiences, perspectives, and strategies.

References

Garrison, D. R., Anderson, T., & Archer, W. (1999). Critical inquiry in a text-based environment: Computer conferencing in higher education. *The Internet and Higher Education, 2*(2–3), 87–105.

Rātima, T. M., Smith, J. P., Macfarlane, A. H., Riki, N. M., Jones, K. L., & Davies, L. K. (2022). Ngā Hau e Whā o Tāwhirimātea: Culturally responsive teaching and learning for the Tertiary Sector.

SPRINGER NATURE

GPSR Compliance

The European Union's (EU) General Product Safety Regulation (GPSR) is a set of rules that requires consumer products to be safe and our obligations to ensure this.

If you have any concerns about our products, you can contact us on ProductSafety@springernature.com

In case Publisher is established outside the EU, the EU authorized representative is:

Springer Nature Customer Service Center GmbH
Europaplatz 3
69115 Heidelberg, Germany

The manufacturer's authorised representative in the EU is Springer Nature Customer Service Centre GmbH, Europaplatz 3, 69115 Heidelberg, Germany. If you have any concerns regarding our products, please contact ProductSafety@springernature.com

Printed and bound by CPI Group (UK) Ltd, Croydon, CR0 4YY

25/03/2026

02078193-0016